A Walk in the Park
Acadia's Hiking Guide
Homans Path - newly restored footpath

Throughout 1991 and 1992 I sought and found many so-called "abandoned trails" on Mount Desert Island. Most were fairly easy to locate; I would view an old map then go to the general spot shown and rummage around for tell-tale signs of an old trail. Only two maps of a series of ten showed this path. It was mentioned in a 1915 guide but not a 1928 guide. It was called the "Homans Path." Finally on a particularly wintry Saturday afternoon in February of 1993, my *Trails of History* writing partner Jay Saunders and I found the upper end of the Homan's Path at a spot where it should not have been.

We were amazed by what we found: a near-fully intact path that had six to eight inches of thick moss overgrowing its entire trailbed. Trees six to eight inches in diameter grew in the pathway; clearly few people (if any at all) had been using this arcane path. Uncovering this abandoned trail assisted us greatly in our understanding of the 'Memorial Paths' built by the Bar Harbor Village Improvement Association in the 1910s.

We notified both Acadia National Park officials and Friends of Acadia. Next we photographed the path in its unrestored condition. We included several pages of information about it in our 1993 publication, *Trails of History*. This book chronicled for the first time the entire history of trails and trail-bulding here on Mount Desert Island.

Well, ten years later the park trail crew has rehabilitated the Homan's Path and connected the *Sieur de Monts* Spring area at its base, and Dorr Mountain's East Face Trail (Hike 1-15) at its high point.

The Homans Path is now part of Acadia's trail system.

It starts just north of the Wild Gardens of Acadia; a new cedar post marks the start of a crushed gray granite footpath that winds from the Hemlock Road to the 'base' of the Homan's Path (see photo below).

Finely crafted granite steps and stairs run from this point as the trail winds its way up the northern edge of the east side of Dorr Mountain. Views of Great Meadow, Frenchman Bay, and Bar Harbor appear. The trail runs through a couple small crevices as it crosses a severe talus slope. The path then turns to the south and runs back to the East Face Trail (a.k.a. the Emery Path). See hike 1-15 for greater description of this area.

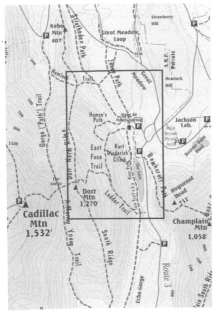

Homan's Path
Approx. Distance: .7 mi
Difficulty Rating: moderate
Technical Challenge: moderate
Notable: Built in 1915; found in 1993; restored in 2003

W9-BHJ-883

INTRODUCTION

A Walk in the Park - Version Ten

A lot has changed since the first version of *A Walk in the Park* came out in 1991. The trail system at Acadia is in the best shape it has been in many years. Moreover, it stands to see its first major overhaul in nearly seventy years with the advent of "Acadia Trails Forever," a massive undertaking to restore the entire trail system by the Park Service and Friends of Acadia. An enormously generous donation by the Colket Family of Bar Harbor has made the whole project possible. Things look great for the trails of Acadia National Park.

Acadia's trail crew (pictured on the inside front cover of this book) restored many trails during the nineties, including the Pond Trail, Beachcroft Path, the Kane Path, Jordan Pond Trail, Ocean Drive Trail, the Precipice, Kurt Diederich's Climb, and Stratheden Path just to name a few. The full list is much longer. The efforts of the trail crew represent the start of this great res-toration project.

There are approximately 110 miles of maintained, marked trails on Mount Desert Island. Virtually every trail in the system is at least eighty years old. Hiking these trails represents a popular pastime for hundreds of thousands of people each year. *A Walk in the Park* provides clear, concise directions to hikes on virtually every trail or path in the system.

There is a reason that this book outsells every other trail guide book: it is the best one. It contains all the trails and carriage roads. It is full of useful information to make your hiking experience at Acadia an enjoyable one. The maps are clear and easy to read. The profile views and the informational boxes on the map page contain lots of valuable data. The text fully describes each hike. The book is routinely updated. It is written by the person with the most knowledge of the trail system. Need I say more?

O.K. you want more? The book contains coupons worth three times the retail price of the book.

I've been planning this revision for several years. As I put the finishing touches on Version Ten of *A Walk in the Park*, I am excited to get this edition to market.

This year's book has been reformatted to fit into your back pocket. I've employed the 'lay-flat' binding but kept extended back covers. I've added a much-needed index. The pages are numbered, and the hikes are cross-refer-enced. The maps are all updated, and I've added lots of new graphical infor-mation to the profile views including net elevation gains and losses, and a valuable piece of data each hike: gross vertical change. I cross-referenced each hike with the Acadia National Park trail crew's field notes for distances.

I've consolidated the photos of the book and attempted to put a picture on each page.

The largest amount of work may show up the least; I polished the text in each hike description while keeping the structure of most hikes the same. I've added lots of subjective value to each hike.

Layout of the Book and a little history

The layout of the book remains the same. Hikes are grouped into five regions, as follows: the Bar Harbor region, the Ocean Drive Region, the Jordan Pond area, Western Mountain, and Somes Sound.

While early versions of the book had roughly the same layout, it turns out that the original trail builders laid out their systems in a similar manner; dif-ferent trail building agencies built hiking trails near their towns and villages. Each community had its own Village Improvement Association or Village Improvement Society that built many of today's trails. I've classified or grouped the trails in the same manner that the original builders cut and built the trails: by their proximity to villages on the island.

The park service formed in 1915. Trail maintenance gradually became the responsibility of the government. By 1926, most VIA or VIS trail work within the park had ceased.

During the 1930s, the Civilian Conservation Corps set up two camps on Mount Desert Island, and a massive restoration project was undertaken. This, however, was to be the final large-scale concerted restoration project until the recent past.

After the fire of 1947, park officials elected to obliterate many trails. In fact, trail mileage dropped from a peak of 260 miles a few years after the CCC's work to today's figure of 110 miles.

Today's Trail System and A Walk in the Park

When *A Walk in the Park* was first published in 1991, the non-profit group Friends of Acadia had undertaken their joint carriage road restoration project with the park service and private donors.

I decided to write a history of the trail system in late 1991 which resulted in the 1993 publication of *Trails of History*, the first ever history book about Mount Desert Island's trails.

The knowledge gained during the research for *Trails of History* has made *A Walk in the Park* a much better book. Historical facts and figures are interspersed throughout the book.

A Walk in the Park has sold well. Many copies have been sold since its inception, and I can hardly believe that this represents the tenth printing of the book.

Acadia Trails Forever & Friends of Acadia

Now, Friends of Acadia has initiated its "Acadia Trails Forever" campaign to restore and permanently endow the hiking trail system at Acadia National Park. The undertaking is massive. It is an 'unprecedented $13-million project...Friends will raise $9 million. The Park Service will commit $4 million.' The objectives: 1) repair, over ten years, Acadia's entire trail system; 2) restore 11 miles of abandoned trails; 3) create five "village connectors," footpaths linking communities to the park; and 4) privately endow the system in perpetuity.

Lead donors Tristram and Ruth Colket of Bar Harbor donated $5 million to start the campaign, the largest monetary gift to a Maine Conservation organization.

The amount of work needed to complete this project has necessitated an expanded trail crew. It has spawned a park service-sponsored gathering of historical information (for which *Trails of History* provided much guidance).

This undertaking can include you. Volunteers are needed, and the park maintains a volunteer coordinator who can be reached at 288.3338.

You may also donate directly to Friends of Acadia. They can be reached via the following: 43 Cottage Street, Bar Harbor, ME 04609. Tel: (207) 288-3340. On the internet at friendsofacadia.org

Parkman Publications

It has been exciting to be involved during such a dynamic time for Acadia's trails.

When I formed Parkman Publications a decade ago, I could never have guessed that my books would chronicle the largest-ever restoration of Acadia's trail system, or that I would have the involvement I do.

I can be reached by the following ways:

Parkman Publications, P.O. Box 826, Bar Harbor, ME 04609

tel: (207) 288-0355

email: tom@bhmaine.com

I welcome your input. The suggestions of many are reflected in this edition, and I've enjoyed all the letters.

A portion of the sale of each book goes directly to the Acadia Trails Forever campaign, and I urge all to donate.   Tom St.Germain

Table of Contents

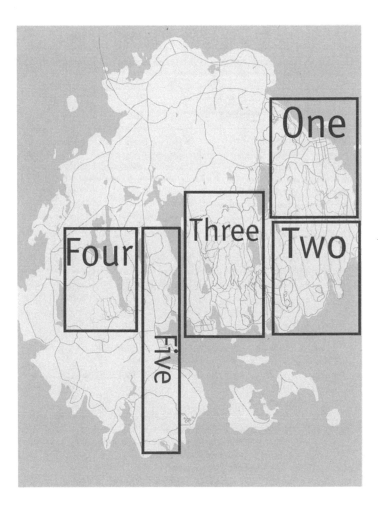

I. The Bar Harbor Region

The Bar Harbor Region contains hikes that range from the easiest to the most difficult. *None of the hikes in this region require you to pass the toll collection station of the park.* The Bar Island hike and the Bar Harbor Shore Path lie within the town's down-town area. Nine of this region's hikes start from the Nature Center/Wild Gardens of Acadia (the park's original hub). The Beachcroft Path climbs the two peaks visible from Main Street in Bar Harbor. Also found in this region is The Precipice, and one of my personal favorites, The Canyon Brook Trail.

Hike	Name	Parking	Level
1-1	Bar Island	in town	easy
1-3	The Shore Path	in town	easy
1-5	Compass Harbor	lot on Rte 3	easy
1-7	Cadillac North Ridge	loop road	difficult
1-9	Kebo Mtn	Nature Center	moderate
1-11	Jesup Path	Nature Center	easy
1-13	Tarn Trail (Kane Path)	Nature Center	moderate
1-15	Kurt Diederich's Climb	Nature Center	difficult
1-17	Dorr Mtn	Nature Center	difficult
1-19	The Gorge Paths	Nature Center	difficult
1-21	The Ladder Trail	south of Tarn	difficult
1-23	Canyon Brook Trail	lot on Rte 3	difficult
1-25	Beachcroft Path	just north of Tarn	difficult
1-27	The Precipice	loop road area	most difficult
1-29	Murphy's Lane	same as Precipice	easy

Compass Harbor parking: approx. one mile south of Bar Harbor on Rte 3; lot with "fire road- do not block" sign on east side of the road.

Cadillac North Ridge: from the Cadillac Mtn Entrance to the park (on Rte 233), proceed toward Cadillac, but go left at the one-way option (toward Sand Beach); parking is on left.

Nature Center: two miles south of Bar Harbor on Rte 3; signs mark Nature Center, Abbe Museum, Sieur de Monts Spring, and Wild Gardens of Acadia.

Ladder Trail: just south of the Tarn, a cairn marks an opening in the bushes.

Canyon Brook Trail: about half a mile further south from Ladder Trail, a cedar post marks the trail from the parking area.

Beachcroft Path: just beyond the Sieur de Monts park entrance, but still north of The Tarn.

Precipice Parking: on one-way section of loop road before the toll booth.

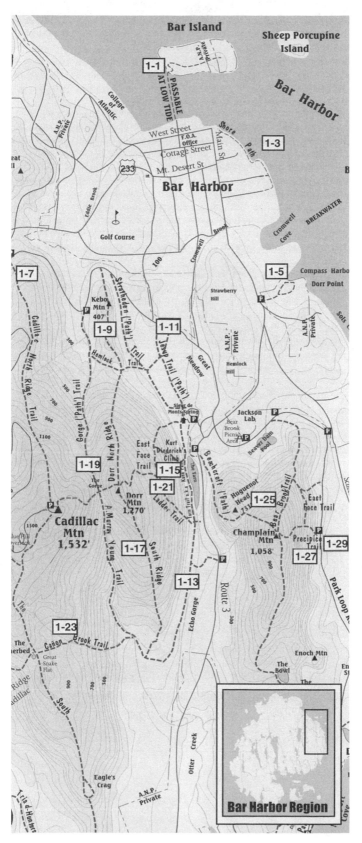

Bar Harbor derives its name from the sand bar that connects it to the first of the Porcupine Islands. The downtown area of Bar Harbor, the sand bar, and the island combine to form the harbor, nestled within Frenchman Bay. More of the bay lies west of the sand bar, but most keeled vessels would risk running aground even at high tide were they to attempt navigation over the bar. The tides average eight to twelve feet between extremes.

At low tide, the sand bar connects the two islands, and dries fully to reveal ruts and tire tracks formed by vehicles passing to Bar Island during previous low tides. Functionally, a road stretches the length of the sand bar. Let all stand warned, however, that only at low tide do the islands connect.

Between tides strong currents will extend the stays of unwatchful visitors to Bar Island. The sand bar lies at the bottom of Bridge Street in town. The Bridge St. extension area provides parking, but the hike really lies in town, making it unnecessary to drive to Bridge Street. Low tide exposes thousands of mussels. To the left, huge mansions dot the shoreline, once known as "Millionaire's Row." Their rocky frontage displays the vertical extent of the tides. Further up the coast the high speed "Cat" docks, and beyond that marina slips appear.

Views extend beyond Hulls Cove along the Frenchman Bay coast. The hike continues: after passing the bar, a fire gate blocks vehicles from proceeding further. However, the park service maintains a trail that rises beyond the gate. Its first section passes through a large field. Well packed grass provides just about ideal footing. Anywhere in the field provides great picnic potential.

After the field, the trail splits. Follow to the left. The grade increases, and the footing deteriorates. Small, loose stones clog the trail temporarily. The good footing returns as the peak approaches. One more small field stands before the top of the trail. At the top, an old flag pole stands in the cairn-like pile of stones marking the island's high point (120 f.a.s.l.). From this point, plenty of sights appear: the downward sloping business district of the town spills over the hill. The Bar Harbor Inn and its pier, the town pier, and various coastal merchants dot the shoreline. Further east, the shore of the bay extends to the unfinished breakwater.

The end of the breakwater connects to Bald Porcupine Island, and Sheep Porcupine Island lies between Bald and Bar Island. The park service owns the western side of this island. The cobble beaches of the north and west side of Bar Island provide interesting exploration and good views in those directions.

Before hiking this route, consult authoritative tide charts!

An old lithograph depicts Bar Harbor in the 1880s, as viewed from Bar Island.

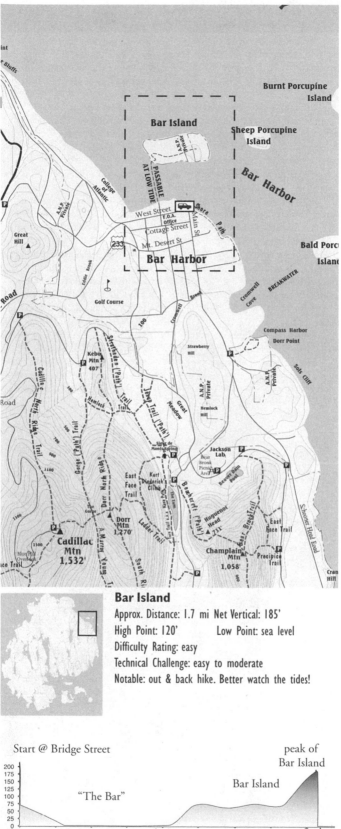

Bar Island

Approx. Distance: 1.7 mi   Net Vertical: 185'

High Point: 120'   Low Point: sea level

Difficulty Rating: easy

Technical Challenge: easy to moderate

Notable: out & back hike. Better watch the tides!

Start @ Bridge Street

peak of
Bar Island

"The Bar"

Bar Island

Bar Island

.4mi   .8mi

The landowners along the shore of Frenchman Bay from the town pier at the intersection of Main and West Streets, and extending along the east shore for almost a mile have provided a nice, easy hike. A path connects their front yards along the water. Their graciousness allows walkers to see the Bar Harbor shoreline.

A paved sidewalk ends at the Bar Harbor Inn pier and patio marking the beginning of the Shore Path. It runs along a sea wall whose sides have endured, for better or worse, repeated thrashings of harsh storms and tides. Past the inn grounds, the path runs along the edge of Albert Meadow, a public park. A sign explains some of the history of the Shore Path near Balance Rock, a huge boulder that sits in shallow water near the shore. The long yard of the Balance Rock Inn leads to one of the island's finest inns.

The Shore Path provides an alternative to watching the sun rises from the top of Cadillac; day breaks over the horizon beyond the Schoodic Peninsula to the east. Ahead, the unfinished breakwater appears and disappears with the tides, connecting to Bald Porcupine Island.

The other Porcupine Islands form a line to the west and north. The fence along the right side of the trail turns, marking the Shore Path's outlet to Bar Harbor, but the path continues ahead a bit before ending. Back in 1990 I spent a great fall living almost alone in the large Tudor Style house near the end of the Shore Path. Needless to say, the house was in different ownership then.

Ahead, Ogden Point juts out between Cromwell Cove and Compass Harbor (hike 1-5) further down the Bar Harbor coast opposite the breakwater.

Hikers can return "down town" by either following the path along the fence alluded to earlier or by retracing the steps back to the inn. The path along the fence comes out on Hancock Street which runs back into Main Street at the Ford dealership.

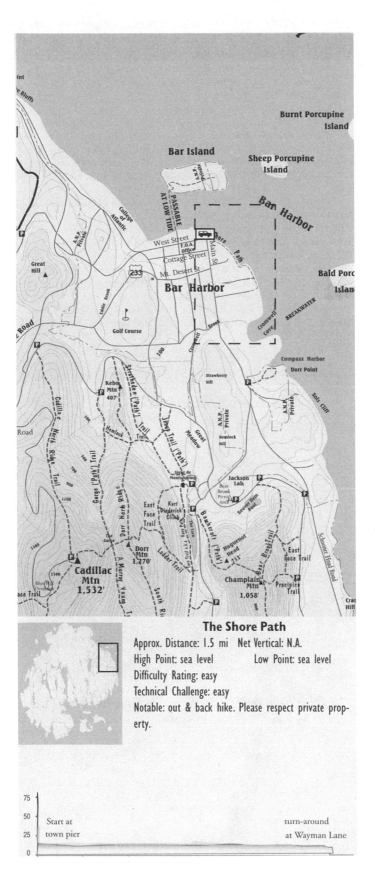

Compass Harbor lies just outside the downtown area of Bar Harbor, close enough to be within walking distance of town (one mile from the intersection of Main and Mt. Desert Streets).

The hike passes through a small area of woods and leads to a tight, rocky harbor. The gravel path leading into the woods from the parking area splits. The hike veers off to the left. Huge trees, obviously spared from the massive 1947 fire have grown old in these woods. The trail stays perfectly flat as it approaches a grassy area and leads up to Dorr Point along the south rim of Compass Harbor. The rocks around the point provide plenty of quiet resting or sunning spots.

The Bar Harbor Breakwater juts off Bald Porcupine Island to the east. Further out, the Schoodic Peninsula area of Acadia stretches into the Atlantic. Walkers can vary their return trip to include an interesting loop through the woods: as you head back, on the left side of the grassy area just away from Dorr Point, a small trail cuts into the woods beyond the large tree. This sand-and dirt-covered trail winds through the woods and reaches a long-since homeless set of granite steps, formerly a part of the summer cottage Old Farm of George B. Dorr, Acadia's founder. Hewn of granite from Echo Gorge between Huguenot Head and Dorr Mountain, Old Farm served as host to various dignitaries including two U.S. Presidents during George Dorr's work in forming the national park.

The trail back continues over and through the foundation. (Ignore the options to go to the left; Dorr, a noted trail designer, built all sorts of paths connecting Old Farm with the park, the town of Bar Harbor, and area landmarks.

The trail bends to the right. Runoff waters have eroded the last few feet of this section of trail, yet it soon rejoins the original path and reaches the parking area about 100 yards later.

The architect's elevation drawing of Old Farm. The actual house was less ornate.

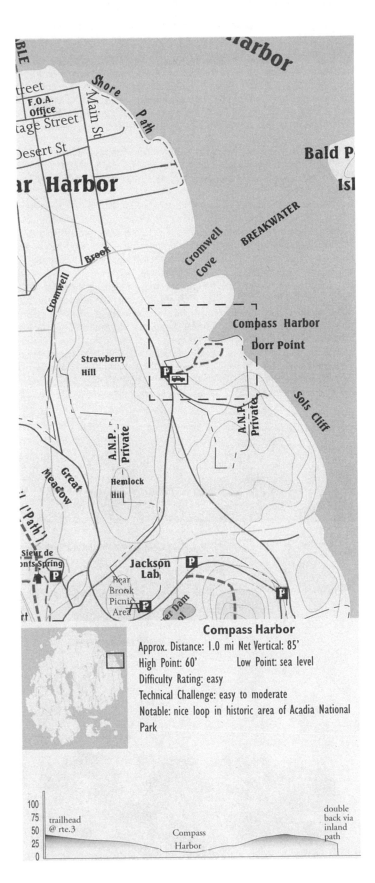

Harbor

Street
F.O.A. Office
tage Street
Desert St

Shore Path
Main St

ar Harbor

Bald P

Isl

BREAKWATER

Cromwell Cove

Cromwell Brook

Cromwell

Compass Harbor
Dorr Point

Strawberry Hill

P

Sols Cliff

A.N.P. Private

A.N.P. Private

Great Meadow

Hemlock Hill

[Path]

Sieur de nts Spring
P

Jackson Lab

P

Bear Brook Picnic Area

P

er Dam

P

rf

Compass Harbor
Approx. Distance: 1.0 mi   Net Vertical: 85'
High Point: 60'   Low Point: sea level
Difficulty Rating: easy
Technical Challenge: easy to moderate
Notable: nice loop in historic area of Acadia National Park

100
75   trailhead
50   @ rte.3
25
0

Compass Harbor

double back via inland path

13

CADILLAC MTN NORTH RIDGE
TRAIL a moderately difficult hike up Cadillac

The North Ridge trail up Cadillac starts off the loop road near the Rte 233 entrance (the Cadillac Mtn entrance) to Acadia. Instead of taking a right toward Jordan Pond and Cadillac, take a left onto the start of the one way road. A cedar post marks the North Ridge Trail on the right. A parking area on the left overlooks Bar Harbor, the Porcupine Islands, and Frenchman Bay.

After jumping up from the loop road, the trail starts over smooth rock and follows the historically interesting route (approximately) of the old rough buckboard road up the mountain. Eagle Lake appears to the west. (This nubble of Cadillac was formerly known as Great Pond Hill, and Eagle Lake was known as Great Pond.)

Slightly higher elevations give good views of Dorr Mt. and the gorge separating it from Cadillac to the east. The trail climbs steadily over smooth rock. It enters a wooded area briefly and steps rock to rock up a fairly steep area. Past the small hardwoods, the trail starts onto the first of two broad knolls on the north face of Cadillac. Wide visibility shows the bald mountain side above, and broader vistas of the sights visible from lower heights.

The auto road running up Cadillac converges on the trail about a third of the way up. The trail curves close to two or three roadside parking areas, but each time shies away. However, the sound of straining engines heading up the mountain and the stench of burning break pads slowing the trip down remind hikers of the trail's proximity to the road. The trail veers away from the road and pushes steeply upward in a prolonged, straight path. Water and electrical pipes appear in places, but don't follow them: stay on the trail, marked by cairns and splotches of blue paint. Near the top, the trail levels and swerves around trees and larger rocks. The trail reaches the top near the gift shop.

Revelers celebrate the "First Light" of the new millennium on January 1, 2000.
Hundreds made it to the top of Cadillac in search of a glimpse of the first sunrise of the new year.

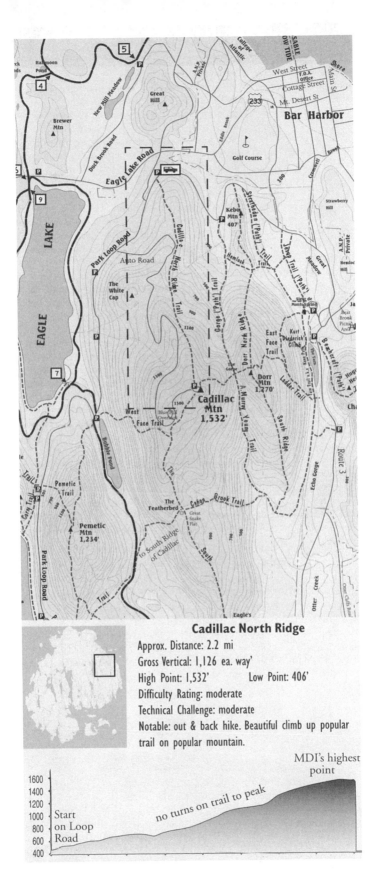

Cadillac North Ridge

Approx. Distance: 2.2 mi

Gross Vertical: 1,126 ea. way'

High Point: 1,532'   Low Point: 406'

Difficulty Rating: moderate

Technical Challenge: moderate

Notable: out & back hike. Beautiful climb up popular trail on popular mountain.

Kebo Mountain occupies a fairly central location but remains virtually anonymous these days, although in the travel books of one-hundred years ago or so Kebo Mountain was viewed as a must hike by many guides.[1]

The small mountain rises only to 407 feet above sea level, but offers good 360° views. away from the top (small trees near the peak make panoramic views from that point difficult. The hike described here consists of three different trail segments and forms a loop that shows off these good views and the nice local topography. The best start of this hike begins from the Nature Center parking near the Sieur de Monts Spring entrance to Acadia.

Proceed past the single measure of fence that blocks the fire road at the north corner of the lot. This road crosses the Jesup Path. About two-tenths of a mile later, the fire road intersects with the Hemlock Trail, marked by a cedar post. Look closely at the flat faced rock that marks the other side of the trail from the cedar post; an inscription here reads "STRATH EDEN PATH," and a newer post marks the 'Strath Eden Trail' in the woods.

Take this right onto Strath Eden. Restored in the early '90s after years of abandonment, Strath Eden runs to the loop road through a grove of young hardwoods.[2] Follow the trail straight ahead. It runs pleasantly along a shelf on the southwest side of Kebo Mtn, crossing several bridges and other old, abandoned paths and roads.

The trail reaches the loop road at an unmarked parking area. Follow the loop road to the left for 100 yards. Here, a new cedar post marks the North Ridge Trail up Dorr Mtn. Follow this trail to the left: it rises abruptly away from the loop road and to the top of Kebo Mountain. Kebo contains two small peaks, separated by a small dip. Good views of the golf course, some residential areas of Bar Harbor, and the Great Meadow appear. Other vistas include Frenchman Bay from north to east, as well as good views of Dorr and Cadillac including the gorge between the two peaks. The relatively long south ridge of Kebo Mtn gradually drops toward the aforementioned Hemlock Trail.

The surface varies, but generally provides easy walking. The hike reaches the Hemlock Trail at a sign post that points to the Gorge Path to the right, up Dorr Mtn straight ahead, and back to Sieur de Monts Spring to the left. Follow to the left. The trail drops in gradual spurts over different types of rocky surfaces and returns to the fire road that began the hike at the rock bearing the Strath Eden inscription. The parking area lies three-tenths of a mile to the right.

Addendum: the Great Meadow Loop

Built as part of Friends of Acadia's Village Trail Connectors initiative, the Great Meadow Loop connects Acadia's trail system to the outer edge of Bar Harbor. The Great Meadow Loop starts up Kebo Street (shown on this map), runs parallel to Kebo Street, bends to the east along the loop road, passes the northern end of the Jesup Path (hike 1-11), then crosses the so-called Ledgelawn Extension (also known as Great Meadow Drive), and runs along that road back toward the border between Acadia National Park and Bar Harbor.

This trail is shown on this map.

---

1. In the days before the golf course, travel guides recommended taking the Harden Farm Road to the old mill at Kebo Brook. Remnants of some of these paths and roads can still be found today, but no sign of the mill exists.

2. Originally known as the Harden Farm Road, George Dorr rebuilt the path and called it Strath Eden. With it, he connected the town of Bar Harbor with the spring (at Sieur de Monts) which he bought and made into the original Sieur de Monts National Monument.

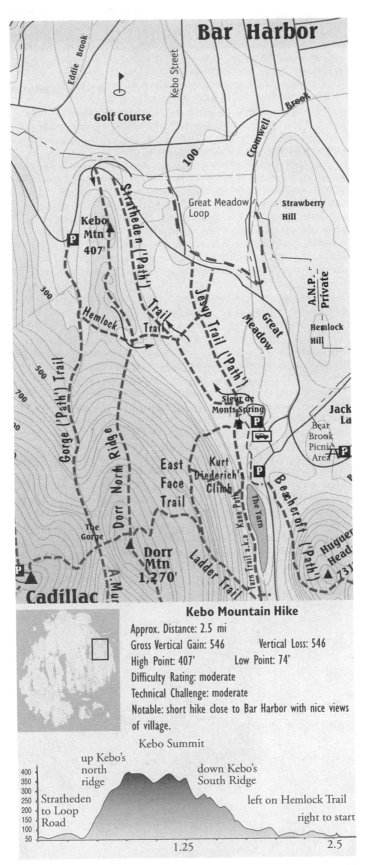

Bar Harbor

Eddie Brook
Kebo Street
Cromwell Brook

Golf Course

100

Kebo Mtn 407'

Stratheden ("Path") Trail

Great Meadow Loop

Strawberry Hill

Hemlock Trail

Jesup Trail ("Path")

Great Meadow

A.N.P. Private

Hemlock Hill

300

Gorge ("Path") Trail

500
700

Dorr North Ridge

Sieur de Monts Spring

Jack La

Bear Brook Picnic Area

East Face Trail

Kurt Diederich's Climb

Kane Path

The Tarn

Beachcroft ("Path")

The Gorge

A.Mur

Dorr Mtn 1,270'

Ladder Trail

Tarn Trail a.k.a. Kane Path

Huguer Head 731

Cadillac

Kebo Mountain Hike

Approx. Distance: 2.5 mi
Gross Vertical Gain: 546   Vertical Loss: 546
High Point: 407'   Low Point: 74'
Difficulty Rating: moderate
Technical Challenge: moderate
Notable: short hike close to Bar Harbor with nice views of village.

Kebo Summit

up Kebo's north ridge

down Kebo's South Ridge

Stratheden to Loop Road

left on Hemlock Trail

right to start

400
350
300
250
200
150
100
50

1.25   2.5

The Jesup Path occupies the large tract of land extending from the loop road near the Kebo Valley Golf Club, across the Great Meadow and past the Nature Center and Sieur de Monts Spring to the north end of the Tarn where it connects to the Kane Path (called the Tarn Trail today).

When built, the Jesup Path extended into the downtown area of Bar Harbor, effectively connecting the town to the park. Today, Friends of Acadia has spearheaded an effort that connects the Jesup Path with a 'Village Trail Connector' across the loop road from the northern end of the Jesup Path.

The Jesup Path provides fertile ground to bird watchers, and to all others it stands as a nice walk in the woods because it is well maintained by different trail maintenance agencies. The end of the parking lot farthest from the Nature Center provides access to the Jesup Path. A lone section of wooden fence blocks the entrance to the gravel path. The Jesup Path crosses this gravel path just beyond the gardens. Follow the trail to the right through the multitude of birches. The rich, moist soil of the trail appears dark against the green grass and white birches, and the park service has constructed an extended bog walk through this wet area. Beyond the bog walk, the surface feels spongy underfoot.

Slanting sun rays form complex geometric shadows as they pass through the trees. The trail reaches the end of this grove and meets the lowland known as The Great Meadow, a freshwater marsh.

Take a right, following the course of the old Great Meadow Fire Truck Trail.[1] Growth of local vegetation, nourished by the waters of the marsh, can quickly obscure the path. A section of cement provides solid footing beneath a small stream across the trail. The trail reaches the loop road across from the golf course at an unmarked parking area. Take a left and walk along the loop road for 100 yards. A cedar post marks the Jesup Path on the left. Follow this narrow trail. After crossing several bridges, the path runs along a miniature berm of dry land through the marsh. It connects back to the birch area where hikers can head back along the path through the birches or follow the trail to the right and return along the fire road properly known as the Hemlock Road.

To add another short flat loop to the hike, take a right back onto the Jesup Path before it reaches the parking area. The trail runs behind the Wild Gardens and the Nature Center, then in front of the Abbe Museum. It crosses a small foot bridge, and reaches the north end of the Tarn about a quarter mile from the gardens. Here a bronze plaque serves as a memorial to the Jesups.

A left over the three stones that span the flow of water out of The Tarn, followed by another left at a cedar post, leads down granite stairs and brings hikers to a short, level trail that stretches back toward the parking area. Also restored by the CCC in the 1930s, this trail was abandoned until recently, but it now connects back to the Nature Center.

Most of the trails on this hike are not on other maps!!!

A glimpse of the mess caused by beavers at the north end of the Tarn.

---

1. Built by the Civilian Conservation Corps during the 1930s, it was designed as a fire fighting tool.

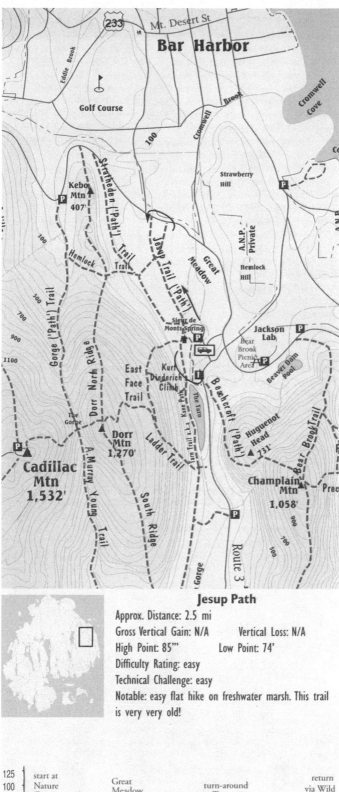

Jesup Path

Approx. Distance: 2.5 mi

Gross Vertical Gain: N/A   Vertical Loss: N/A

High Point: 85'"   Low Point: 74'

Difficulty Rating: easy

Technical Challenge: easy

Notable: easy flat hike on freshwater marsh. This trail is very very old!

125	start at			return
100	Nature	Great	turn-around	via Wild
75	Center	Meadow	at Tarn	Gardens path
50				
25				

THE TARN TRAIL (KANE PATH[1]) a
moderate, rolling hike along inland waters

The Kane Path covers all sorts of ground, and signs call it different things depending on its direction. This hike describes its basically flat trek behind The Tarn, where different signs refer to it as the Jesup Path, the Tarn Trail, Canon Brook Trail, as well as two old signs that call it The Kane Path.

From the lot at Sieur de Monts Spring walk past the Nature Center and follow the sidewalk toward the Abbe Museum. Take a left over the small foot bridge and follow the trail into woods. The trail reaches the north end of The Tarn and continues along the pond's back side. Here, an etching proves that some things are written in stone. A bronze plaque also denotes the trail's proper name: The Kane Path.[2]

Clear and straightforward, the trail runs as close to any water's edge as a trail can. Flat stones, inches above the level of the water, create the treadway. More flat stones, nicely forming the trail over and between much larger stones, continue ahead. [3] Trail crews have restored the trail nicely along the southern end of The Tarn.

Stay to the right over the rocks and know that it is only a short section; the obscurity clears soon, presenting a twisting, rocky trail. Otter Creek runs through Beaver Brook Valley and reaches the ocean a few miles later. The Kane Path passes the Ladder Trail just south of The Tarn.

Otter Creek, swampy in places, crawls through the woods on the right. The waters of the creek and the runoff from the mountain can combine to dampen the ground in the area. The trail slices classically through the woods.[4] Excellent footing, occasionally interrupted by small rocks, cover its length. Well packed dirt, often covered by leaves, lines the trail between the many small bridges that span mountain runoffs. Grass and saplings grow on both sides. Hardwood trees, especially beech and birch, dominate the woods. Beavers live in the creek on the left (further south, away from the trail, the beavers trim local woods).

Away from The Tarn, the trail starts to roll. The gyrations start small, but their frequency and size increase, giving the hike a roller coaster effect. Area birds use the trail as a channel, and fog uses the waters of the creek to creep inland. South of this trail, starting at the park loop road where Otter Creek passes under the road, fog follows the waters of Otter Creek with remarkable accuracy. Thick fog often fills the space above the creek while the Kane Path stays clear as day. Wisps of fog can add to the Sleepy Hollow atmosphere on foggy days.[5] The trail leaves the creek's edge and rises in earnest for the first time over a gravel-like surface. After the brief rise, it passes the Dorr Mtn South Ridge Trail on the right, and eases toward the end of its flatness at the intersection with the Gorge Path and the trail to Eagle's Crag (on Cadillac's South Ridge) which begins the Canyon Brook Trail, and is discussed fully in hike 1-23!

---

1. *The Kane Path's* name was superseded by the name *The Tarn Trail.*

2. Designed by George Dorr and built as part of the Bar Harbor VIA's Memorial Paths, Mrs. John Innes Kane commissioned the construction of the route as a memorial to her husband. The Kanes donated heavily to the Hancock County Trustees of Public Reservation, the group that formed Acadia.

3. One particular stair case along this path formerly bore the name "The Gates of Eden." The woods beyond were known as *Eden Woods* during the island's busiest period of path building; all these facts are presented fully in the book *Trails of History.*

4. The Kane Path was one of the first long loops I ever did on Mount Desert Island, with a park map folded under my runner geek's watch, showing trails with no names, making me realize the need for a good guide!

5. When I'm feeling superstitious or paranoid (which is often), I could swear this trail is haunted.

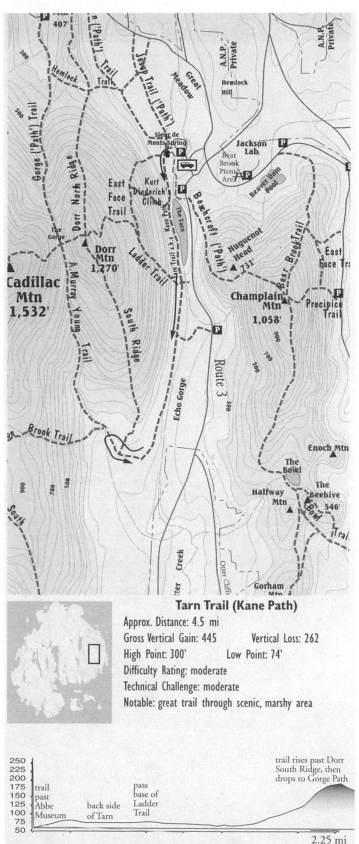

Tarn Trail (Kane Path)

Approx. Distance: 4.5 mi

Gross Vertical Gain: 445   Vertical Loss: 262

High Point: 300'   Low Point: 74'

Difficulty Rating: moderate

Technical Challenge: moderate

Notable: great trail through scenic, marshy area

trail rises past Dorr South Ridge, then drops to Gorge Path

trail past Abbe Museum

back side of Tarn

pass base of Ladder Trail

250 225 200 175 150 125 100 75 50

2.25 mi

Many trails in the vicinity of Dorr Mtn contain stone stairs as their major element. Hundreds and hundreds of heavy duty granite stairs make walking these trails a pleasure. The layout of the trails allow them to skirt the edge of the mountain face, efficiently covering steep ground. The trails described in this hike make climbing one of the steepest mountain faces on the island just another walk in the park.

To get to the start of Kurt Diederich's Climb head toward the Abbe Museum from the Nature Center. Take a left on the foot bridge on the left side of the sidewalk. The trail runs to the north end of The Tarn and intersects with the Diederich Climb on the right. The words "Kurt Diederich's Climb" are inscribed in the first set of stairs rising away from The Tarn.

The stair step pattern begins almost immediately, and good views to both the north and the south appear soon as well. Hikers should take care to stay on the stone steps and ramps in this first section. Hiking along the side of these stairs has eroded much of the lower edges of the trail. As an historical note, this trail was built in 1913 without rock coping; the absence of the coping allows hikers to walk on the trail's edges although hikers should take care to preserve this historically important path by walking along its intended treadway!

During many of the cutbacks along the Diederich Climb the flat sections of connected rocks provide a virtually flat walking surface. Built across a talus field[2] the trail requires a stepped style. Kurt Diederich's Climb intersects with the Dorr Mtn East Face Trail after half a mile of hiking, and continues up to the left.[3] Overlooks appear more often from the trail as it rises from rock to rock. The best views are of The Tarn straight below, the Great Meadow's eastern edge just north, and Bar Harbor and Frenchman Bay further north.

The trail meets with the Ladder Trail and continues up to the right along the East Face Trail. Only a few more stairs remain as the trail traverses the dome of Dorr Mtn over smooth rock. Several unique cairns form arches as they mark the trail. Hikers reach the Dorr Mtn trail crossroads before reaching the actual mountain summit. The top of the mountain lies just to the left. I recommend returning via the East Face Trail, passing the Ladder Trail and reaching the intersection with the Diederich Climb. Follow the trail to the left at this sign post. This stepped trail contains even more history than the Diederich Climb. Like the Diederich Climb, this path was designed and constructed under the supervision of George B. Dorr. The CCC restored the Emery Path in 1935, adding coping, nine rock culverts, several drains below the surface of the trail, and many other hidden aspects.

After writing Trails of History during 1992 and 1993, I became obsessed with the east face of Dorr Mountain and would climb the trails along Sieur de Mont's Crag two or three times a day every day. I never get tired of the views as the trail drops from the intersection along the East Face Trail back to the parking area at the Wild Gardens.

This 1916 picture shows Kurt Diederich's daughter on the path named for him (from *Trails of History*.

---

1. The East Face Trail's proper name is the Emery Path; built by George Dorr and paid for by the widow of John S. Emery during 1913, the Emery Path was a favorite of Mr. Dorr and therefore, a well-known and oft-hiked trail.

2. A talus field is a geological term referring to a rock slide pattern of angular fragments of boulders, usually lying at the base of cliffs.

3. From this intersection, proper names of the trail to the left is the Schiff Trail, and to the right, the Emery Path; now both bear the name *East Face Trail*.

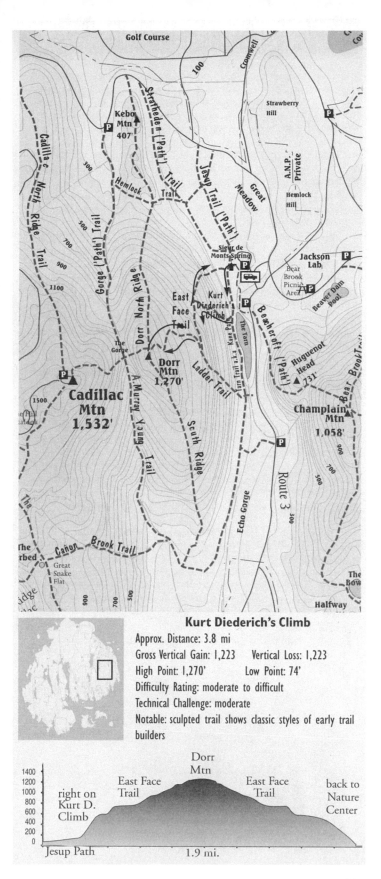

Golf Course

Cromwell

Strawberry Hill

Kebo Mtn 407'

Stratheden ['Path'] Trail

Jesup Trail ['Path']

Great Meadow

A.N.P. Private

Hemlock Hill

Hemlock Trail

Cadillac North Ridge Trail

Gorge ('Path') Trail

Jackson Lab

Sieur de Monts Spring

Bear Brook Picnic Area

Beaver Dam Pool

Dorr North Ridge

East Face Trail

Kurt Diederich's Climb

The Kane Path ['Path']

The Tarn

Beachcroft ['Path']

Huguenot Head 731'

The Gorge

Dorr Mtn 1,270'

Ladder Trail

A. Murray Young Trail

Cadillac Mtn 1,532'

Champlain Mtn 1,058'

South Ridge

Route 3

Echo Gorge

The rbed

Canon Brook Trail

Great Snake Flat

The Bow

Halfway

Kurt Diederich's Climb

Approx. Distance: 3.8 mi
Gross Vertical Gain: 1,223   Vertical Loss: 1,223
High Point: 1,270'   Low Point: 74'
Difficulty Rating: moderate to difficult
Technical Challenge: moderate
Notable: sculpted trail shows classic styles of early trail builders

Dorr Mtn

East Face Trail — East Face Trail

right on Kurt D. Climb

back to Nature Center

1400 1200 1000 800 600 400 200 0

Jesup Path — 1.9 mi.

Dorr Mountain remains a forgotten little brother of Cadillac. And as if having the island's highest peak overshadowing it to the west weren't enough, the popular Champlain Mountain, home of the Precipice Trail, lies to the east. Dorr Mt. remains quiet & little used.

No less than six trails start from lower heights toward the top of Dorr. From the far corner of the parking area, follow the gravel path blocked by the single section of fence. The path runs along the Wild Gardens to the left and the beginning of the Great Meadow to the right. After about three tenths of a mile, a weathered cedar post marks The Hemlock Trail to the left. At the intersection that immediately follows, take a left. The trail rises steep and straight over various forms of footing. It drops as it reaches a signpost marking the intersection with the Kebo Mountain Trail and Dorr's North Ridge Trail. Take a left up the Dorr Mtn trail.

Tiny Kebo Mountain blocks some of the view directly to the north, but to the northeast Bar Harbor, the Porcupine Islands, Frenchman Bay and its north shore appear. The trail continues its steep, steady rise. The top of Dorr lies deceptively far from the end of the steep pitch. The Dorr Mtn crossroads marks the joining of all the trails up Dorr, but the mountain's summit lies further ahead. Once there, a cedar post marks the top. To the west, tourists appear ant-like as they roam the top of Cadillac, spilling over the pseudo-sidewalks on that peak. The west face of Dorr drops sharply into the gorge shared by the two peaks.

More views appear to the north, and the ocean pops up behind Champlain. The South Ridge Trail allows appreciation of the southern exposure. Proceed down the south ridge. The trail runs along the spine of the ridge, offering views over both steep edges.

To the right the long South Ridge of Cadillac stretches, with various streams visibly running down its side. To the left the rocky back side of Champlain appears. Straight ahead the winding pattern of Otter Creek collects run-off from all sides and heads to the sea while often serving as an avenue for fog. The trail drops mostly over smooth rock broken by stretches of soft dirt. Stone-marked, the trail can become difficult to follow, although all of the mountain was repainted in 1991 and again in 1992 (this time with blue paint). The South Ridge Trail ends and intersects with the Kane Path (see hike 1-13).

Follow the trail to the left. After rolling for a while, the trail flattens and runs the length of Dorr's low eastern side and cuts behind The Tarn. Flat rocks provide easy footing, although some naughty little beavers have tried since '94 to build a dam at the north end of The Tarn, causing the trail to fall under water. Funny thing though, the little dam keeps getting washed out.

The Nature Center and the Wild Gardens parking area lie a short distance from the end of The Tarn, accessible either by following the Jesup Path straight ahead, or by taking a right across the stepping stones on the north end of The Tarn, then a quick left at the cedar post.

The giant cairn that
sits atop
Dorr Mountain

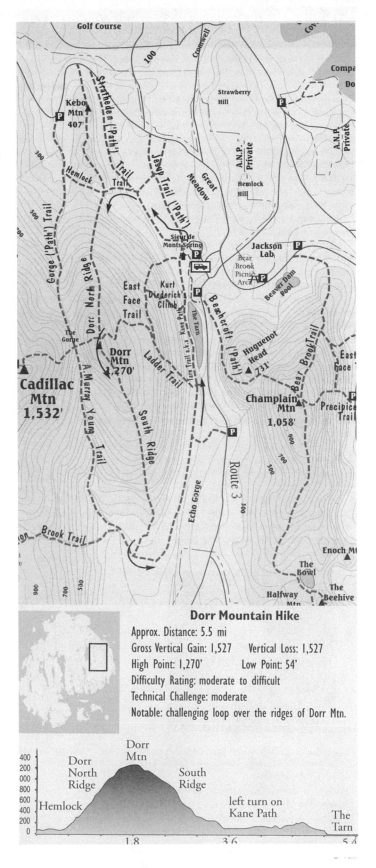

Dorr Mountain Hike

Approx. Distance: 5.5 mi

Gross Vertical Gain: 1,527   Vertical Loss: 1,527

High Point: 1,270'   Low Point: 54'

Difficulty Rating: moderate to difficult

Technical Challenge: moderate

Notable: challenging loop over the ridges of Dorr Mtn.

This is one of my favorite loops. While circling Dorr Mtn, the course includes a bit of everything. The hike starts along the Jesup Path that crosses between the back of the Nature Center and the front of the Abbe Museum and Sieur de Monts Spring. It leads into the woods from the foot bridge in front of the museum and white gazebo. The hike follows the (extreme) back edge of The Tarn along the Kane Path where it runs just inches from water level in some areas. The trail levels over the next 1.5 miles.

The swampy Otter Creek parallels the trail as it runs along the base of Dorr Mtn. After rising away from the creek, the trail drops gradually, passing the south ridge trail up Dorr, and meeting two other trails and two mountain brooks at the same intersection. Follow the (Murray) Gorge Path Trail to the right. Signs mark a course toward Cadillac Mtn. (1.7 mi.), & Dorr Mtn (1.5 mi.). I always consider it my high privilege to do this section of trail, and it is especially beautiful in the fall.[1]

The water gurgles loudly through the steep sided valley. The steady but sure rise over staircases continues. The trail opens to a clearing, covering alternating surfaces of grass and stone as it heads toward the low point of the U-shaped valley ahead.[2]

Higher elevations require rock-to-rock climbing. The trail carefully picks its way to the top of the valley, known as The Notch, showing steep mountain sides to the left and right and views of the ocean to the south. Short but steep detours up the Notch Trails to Cadillac on the left and Dorr on the right begin from this point. This hike continues straight ahead, however.

Heading down now, the trail drops almost immediately into another gorge, this one much deeper. Its north to south orientation and deep walls keep the trail cool even on the hottest days. The thirty to forty foot walls provide insulation. The depth of the gorge produces condensation, and a stream runs along the base as well, wetting the trail's surface and making footing slippery in places.

Lower, the gorge fades but the trail shares the same course with Kebo Brook. When the trail levels, the hike reaches the only signpost on the trail as it heads down.[3] Cross the stream at this sign and head toward Sieur de Monts and Kebo Mountain (along what is known as the Hemlock Trail).

Mostly round stones cover the trail below tall grass. The trail passes the Dorr Mtn North Ridge Trail on the right, and Kebo Mtn on the left, and then drops in a fairly steep, steady descent to a gravel path, formerly known as the Hemlock Road. Follow the Hemlock Road to the right. The parking lot lies about three tenths of a mile from this last intersection.

A granite bridge spans the Gorge Path near the loop road

---

1. Built under the direction of Bar Harbor VIA path chairman Harold Peabody, the paths of The Gorge and Canyon Brook have proved to be among the most durable on the island.

2. Beaver activity has forced the abandonment of some 200 stepping stones in this area where the trail curves to the left over the grassy area.

3. You may notice bronze plaques attached to large stones in both the south gorge, a memorial to A. Murray Young, and the north gorge, a memorial to Lilian Endicott Francklyn.

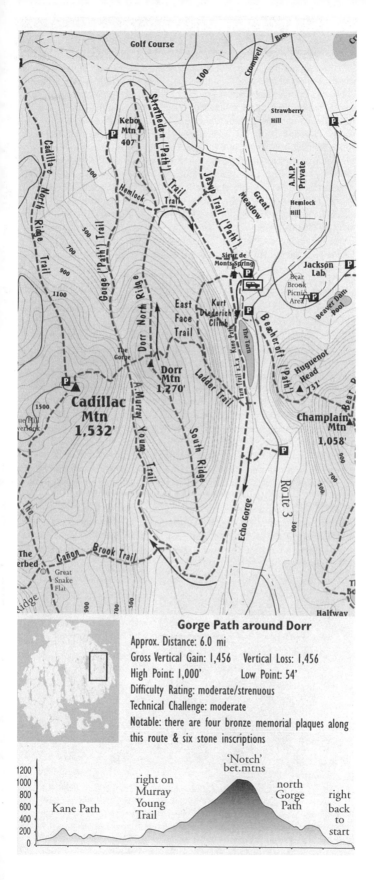

Gorge Path around Dorr

Approx. Distance: 6.0 mi

Gross Vertical Gain: 1,456   Vertical Loss: 1,456

High Point: 1,000'   Low Point: 54'

Difficulty Rating: moderate/strenuous

Technical Challenge: moderate

Notable: there are four bronze memorial plaques along this route & six stone inscriptions

Dorr Mountain's Ladder Trail stands as one of the island's oldest and most exquisite trails. Built in 1893 by the father of Acadia's trail system, Waldron Bates, the CCC restored and rebuilt this trail in the early 1930s.

Closed for many years, the Ladder Trail was reopened in 1974. Among the island's most notable trails in terms of design and layout, the Ladder Trail makes traversing one of the island's steepest mountain faces a pleasurable climb. No sign post mark the trail from Route 3. You must park and walk through the opening in the bushes just south of the Tarn.[1] (Alternative starting areas include either the Canyon Brook Trail parking area, two-tenths of a mile further south along Rte 3 or the Tarn parking area at the Beachcroft Path at the north end of the Tarn.)

Granite lines both sides of the Ladder Trail as it crosses the small stream and the Kane Path (see 1-13). The stair step pattern begins immediately inside the woods, and between the current and abandoned sections of the Ladder Path, more than 1,200 stone steps and ramps form the treadway of this trail.

The Ladder Trail contains three ladders that provide safe passage over the several formidable boulders. Stairs constitute over ninety percent of this trail's treadway until in meets the East Face Trail. From there, the trail contains only sporadic steps.[2]

Bar Harbor appears to the north beyond the eastern edge of the Great Meadow. Huguenot Head rises due east.

To the south, the Otter Creek Valley stretches to the ocean. The trail rises to the crossroads near the summit of Dorr Mtn. The peak lies a scant jaunt to the left. The South Ridge Trail is the only trail that starts from the Dorr Mtn summit. It provides a nice way to return to your car. It drops along the south ridge, marked by blue paint and small cairns, giving super views of the valleys to the south for its entire length. The South Ridge Trail ends at an intersection with the Kane Path (see hike 1-13).

Follow the trail to the left from the sign post. It drops sharply at first, then settles into a rolling pattern for the next mile. It borders along the "creeky" part of Otter Creek, and many forms of wildlife often appear in this area.

The trail passes a sign post at an old beaver dam marking Canyon Brook parking. Continue straight ahead, however. Soon, the sign marking the Ladder Trail appears on the left, and the car lies just to the right.

Sculpted granite runs from route 3 to the base of the Ladder Trail

1. A small cairn marks this opening; although the CCC's Ladder Trail entrance was nothing short of extravagant; additionally, a nine-foot wide fire truck trail was built southward into Beaver Brook Valley from the Ladder Trail entrance (before the idea of *State Route 3* was even conceived).

2. There is an abandoned section of the original 1893 Ladder Trail that still runs to the top of Dorr Mountain, containing hundreds of stairs.

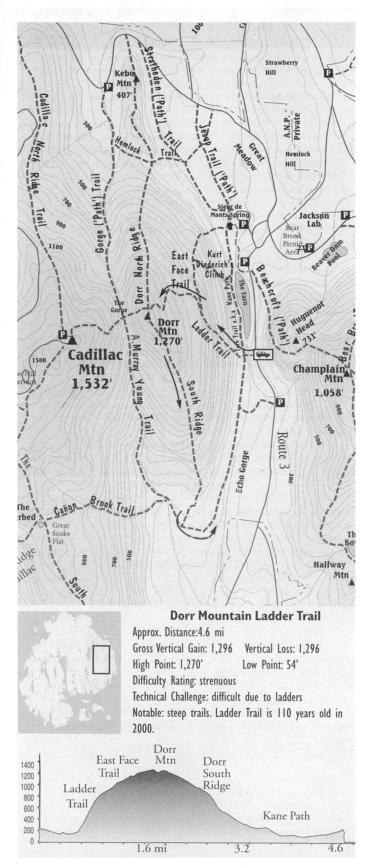

Dorr Mountain Ladder Trail

Approx. Distance: 4.6 mi

Gross Vertical Gain: 1,296   Vertical Loss: 1,296

High Point: 1,270'   Low Point: 54'

Difficulty Rating: strenuous

Technical Challenge: difficult due to ladders

Notable: steep trails. Ladder Trail is 110 years old in 2000.

Parking is provided on the gravel turnoff on the right side of Route 3 where a cedar post marks the trail and a paved parking area forms a semi-circle on the left. This parking area is .3 mi. south of The Tarn.

The trail opens into the birches and beeches, crosses an antiquated beaver dam, and connects to the Kane Path described in 1-13. Of the eight ways to reach the top of Cadillac Mt., Canyon Brook covers the most varied terrain and stands as my favorite trail on the east side of the island. In fact, there was a time in my life when I would run this route every Sunday at twilight.

Combined with the Kane Path, Canyon Brook changes in many ways over its three mile plus course. From the old dam take a left. Roots clog the footing but the grade stays flat. The trail begins to gyrate as the footing improves. After leaving the side of Otter Creek the trail rises, continuing to hug the eastern edge of Dorr Mt. After passing the south ridge trail of Dorr (see hike 1-17), the trail drops to a busy intersection where three trails and two brooks meet.

Follow the signs directing hikers toward Eagle's Crag (2.4 mi) to the left (although this hike does not go as far south as Eagle's Crag). The trail now parallels Canyon Brook. The trail cuts diagonally, right to left up a rough, steep staircase, crossing the brook over this distance.

Clear of this obstacle, the trail changes again. It now rises unlike any other trail or path on Mount Desert Island. It follows the same path as the waters flowing over the smooth rock bed of the brook. Small waterfalls and pools below them occasionally interrupt the smooth flow of water. The trail shares the open brook's path until the smooth rocks fade. Cairns and small splotches of blue paint mark the trail's return to the woods.

After the smooth rock ends a series of stepping stones form the trail as it parallels Canyon Brook for the final time. The hike makes a very tricky left turn across the brook so pay close attention for this turn that crosses the brook.

The stepping stones resume, and after a quarter mile of stair to stair rising, the trail intersects with Cadillac's South Ridge trail at The Featherbed, a small pond in a mountain dimple, called a glacial cirque. Follow the ridge trail to the right. After the brief steep stretch starting the intersection the remainder of the long, gradual incline to the top appears ahead. Broad views in all other directions get better with each step. The South Ridge trail nears the auto road at the Blue Hill overlook then drops back into the woods and ends behind the summit's gift shop. The trip down starts from the east side of Cadillac. The Notch Trail drops steeply due east toward Dorr Mtn.

A brown pine post with white letters directs hikers toward Sieur de Monts and Dorr Mtn. This trail connects the top of Cadillac to the Gorge Path. This post lies on one of the sidewalks next to an illustration overlooking Bar Harbor that talks about summer cottages of yore. Follow the Gorge Path to the right, where the hiking down continues to be difficult, dropping unevenly from rock to rock.

The trail descends over the rocky, wide open glacial valley. A short stretch of grass separates the open valley from the woods. The trail drops as though down a staircase over perfectly laid flat stones. It shares the path of Murray Brook as it drops. The flat stones stretch all the way back to the three-trail-two-brook intersection.

Follow the trail to the left, towards the Tarn and Sieur de Monts Springs. About 1.5 miles later, it rolls by the beaver dam near the parking area on Route 3.

---

1. The trail's proper name is Canyon Brook although current signsuse the word *Canon*. Early explorers thought the split upper south ridge of Cadillac resembled a canyon (which it does). This name became Cañon, and eventually, the *tilde* was lost in transcription from one map to the next.

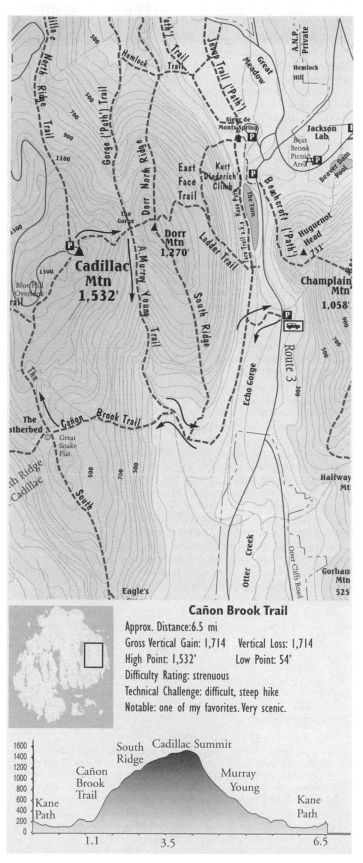

Cañon Brook Trail

Approx. Distance: 6.5 mi

Gross Vertical Gain: 1,714   Vertical Loss: 1,714

High Point: 1,532'   Low Point: 54'

Difficulty Rating: strenuous

Technical Challenge: difficult, steep hike

Notable: one of my favorites. Very scenic.

Champlain and Huguenot Head rise side by side at the north end of MDI's easternmost ridge. They stand in broad view for all to see from Main Street in Bar Harbor. Huguenot Head appears as a perfect dome, connected near its top to the hulking Champlain. Diagonally to the right from the parking area, granite stairs built into the side of Huguenot Head lead to a new cedar post marking the Beachcroft Path.[1]

Built in 1915 as part of the Bar Harbor VIA's Memorial Paths (under the supervision and design of George B. Dorr), the trail curves off to the right after entering the woods. In straight, fairly lengthy stretches the trail cuts back and forth up Huguenot's west side, rounding toward its south side. Flat stones, professionally set by a work crew of six men, provide solid, sure footing. The trail leaves the tree line after a short period in the woods, but underfoot the flat stones continue, well set into the rocky hillside. Most vertical progress occurs at the pivot points of the trail as it cuts back and forth, smoothing a steep trip. Rock retaining and supporting walls have kept this trail in great shape for close to eighty years.

Below, The Tarn empties into Otter Creek, which meanders around the west side of the Champlain ridge until meeting the ocean along the loop road. Due west, the steep, sheer, stark east face of Dorr appears. Once done with the rock to rock hiking, the trail circles around the actual top of Huguenot Head along smooth rock.[2]

The hike up Champlain continues around Huguenot Head on the smooth rock. It drops to where it reaches Champlain's backside, and then rises in earnest. The first stretch presents the greatest challenge of the hike.

Stairs help hikers over the first steep section, but once clear, the remainder of the hike travels over smooth (but steep) stone. The straight up nature of the trail demands hard physical work. Cairns (and sporadic paint splotches) mark the course, but hikers should practice prudent trail watching. Although no trees interfere with views, the effort required makes the hike up the backside mostly an intensive experience.

Spectacular views await at the top. Bar Harbor and the bay sprawl to the north, and the Schoodic Peninsula, the ocean, and Acadia's east coast all appear magnificently from Champlain. The village of Otter Creek appears in the valley behind the mountain, and the Cranberry Isles stretch to the south.

To head down, proceed north toward Bar Harbor, following the Bear Brook Trail. It runs along the north ridge of Champlain, and soon the ugliness of the Jackson Lab appears. Stay left at the only intersection. Smooth stone constitutes most of the footing on Champlain's upper half where the trail falls steadily. Closer to the loop road, the trail levels, and various sized rocks line its path. The trail ends on the loop road next to Beaver Dam Pool. Take a left along the loop road and walk the length of the pond.

With the picnic area on the right, a small cairn marks the trail that connects back to the Beachcroft Path on the left. This short, narrow trail reaches Beachcroft near its start. Follow the trail to the right for the short trip back to the parking area.

---

1. It was the incredible construction of the Beachcroft Path that made me so curious about the history of the trails. In an effort to find out more about Beachcroft, I began the research that became 'Trails of History.' These stairs and the subsequent coping on the lower part of the trail were set by CCC workers some twenty years after the rest of Beachcroft was built.

2. Although poorly marked, a short trail does exist which goes to the top of Huguenot Head. From the smooth rock where the view due south is the best, cairns mark the 150 yard-long trail to Huguenot's peak.

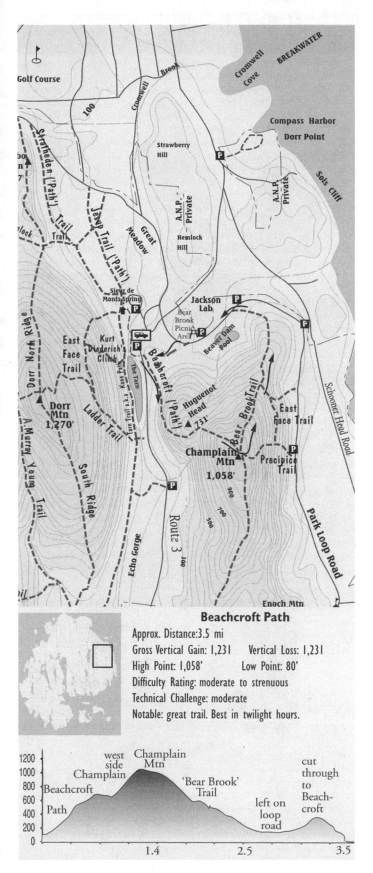

Beachcroft Path

Approx. Distance: 3.5 mi

Gross Vertical Gain: 1,231   Vertical Loss: 1,231

High Point: 1,058'   Low Point: 80'

Difficulty Rating: moderate to strenuous

Technical Challenge: moderate

Notable: great trail. Best in twilight hours.

Perhaps the most popular trail on the island, Precipice is also the most difficult. Climbers should expect an experience physically strenuous and mentally stimulating. Iron ladders and rungs help hikers scale up to twenty vertical feet at a time. The trail constantly teeters along and up the sheer east face of Champlain Mtn. The east side of Champlain, popularly known as the Precipice Trail, stands as an example of Mount Desert Island's basic geographical layout: sheer east and west faces with relatively long, sloping north and south ridges.

From the parking area the hike passes from rock to rock, bends to the right between larger boulders, and encounters a difficult iron rung within 100 yards of the parking area. While tough, this is an indicator of what you can expect higher on this hike. After scaling diagonally across a huge pile of glacial talus, the trail drops, then rises to meet a signpost connecting the Precipice Trail to the East Face Trail[1], the trail I recommend for the descent.

The fun begins after taking a left at the sign. The trail cuts across the face of Champlain, climbing in spurts, falling occasionally, and always offering absolutely straight down views of the area. Higher up, iron rungs and ladders assist hikers over the steepest stretches.[2] The upper portions of this hike require serious physical work, not to mention a bit of mental gumption to skirt what basically amounts to, in places, a cliff. After zigzagging the final stretches of the Precipice, the top appears just beyond yellow metal warning signs. I think the top offers the best views of the Atlantic Ocean and Frenchman Bay from any mountain on the island.

I strongly recommend avoiding a descent on the Precipice Trail, especially since a far better alternative exists, one that involves no backing down over ladders: from the top of Champlain, follow the Bear Brook Trail (Champlain's North Ridge) to the north, towards Bar Harbor. Cairns mark this trail's drop over smooth rock. Soon, the lab appears ahead, and Beaver Dam Pool appears down to the left. At the first sign, take a right.

After a short drop, you will have to choose between dropping straight to the loop road in .2 mi. along the trail to the left, or taking a right along the East Face Trail. The easier option is to drop to the loop road. The East Face Trail assumes stair step characteristics as it runs along the east face of Champlain. A difficult trail in its own right, this trail rises and falls as it skirts the mountain face, but it will bring you back to the first sign you encountered on the trip up. The parking area is visible from this original sign post.

NOTE: dogs should not be brought up The Precipice Trail.

This 1922 picture shows Stephen T. Mather, the Director of the National Park Service, hiking The Precipice. There is also a plaque to Mr. Mather on the top of Cadillac Mtn.

From *Trails of History.*

---

1. Formerly known as the Orange & Black Path, the trail was built by former chairman of the Bar Harbor VIA's path committee, Princeton Prof. Rudolph Brunnow. His school colors were orange and black.

2. The building of The Precipice took years of design and two summers' worth of work for trail crews to construct; see the book *Trails of History* for complete documentation of the construction of this remarkable trail.

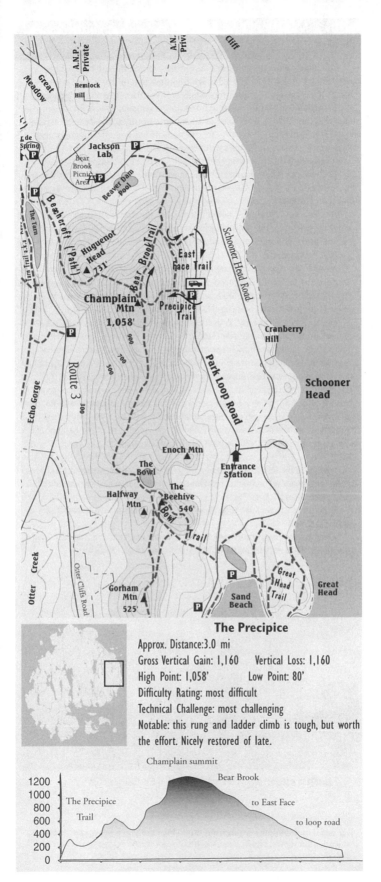

The Precipice

Approx. Distance: 3.0 mi
Gross Vertical Gain: 1,160   Vertical Loss: 1,160
High Point: 1,058'   Low Point: 80'
Difficulty Rating: most difficult
Technical Challenge: most challenging
Notable: this rung and ladder climb is tough, but worth the effort. Nicely restored of late.

This book ranks the Precipice Trail as the most difficult hike on the island, but starting from the same parking area, one of the island's shortest, easiest hikes passes through the swamp on the other side of the loop road.

An unmarked trail runs through the long swamp known as Bliss Field that separates the cliff-like east face of Champlain Mtn from the Atlantic Ocean. Across the loop road, diagonally to the right of the Precipice parking area exit, several stones mark the start of Murphy's Lane.

Originally built by Bar Harbor VIA path chairman Rudolph Brunnow as part of the supporting system to the Precipice Trail construction, this flat trail receives little use today. (The construction of the Precipice Trail pre-dated the loop road along this stretch by over thirty years.)

The trail cuts through a young birch grove and makes a subtle, yet straightforward change in direction. It straightens again as it runs through an oak tree grove and ends at Schooner Head Road, only about a quarter mile from the Precipice lot.

An old trail runs along Schooner Head Road in both directions. Formerly known as the Red Path, there were once plans to connect it to the Ocean Drive Trail; this never happened, and the trail was 'abandoned' once the loop road was built between Sieur de Monts and Sand Beach.

The trail is still in good condition, however. The Schooner Head lookout area lies up the road to the right about six-tenths of a mile. A bit further past the overlook, additional parking with access to both Sand Beach and the Great Head hike exists. Incredible views of the Precipice appear all along Schooner Head Road and provide excellent photo opportunities. The long Champlain south ridge includes Enoch Mtn and The Beehive, visible from Schooner Head Rd. If you do decide to explore along Schooner Head Road in the other direction, when you return don't be fooled by a Murphy's Lane imposter at post number sixty-nine. The proper landmark is the telephone pole across the street from the trail. The numbers on this pole read "3" over "72."

The old Red Path actually runs parallel to Schooner Head Road all the way to the laboratory service entrance (and other trails formerly connected this trail to downtown Bar Harbor).

Hiking along this trail today is a flat, fairly pleasant walk despite its unofficial status.

When returning to the Precipice parking area, watch for the slight right turn about 200 yards into the woods along the old Murphy's Lane.

Champlain rises across Bliss Field west of the old 'Red Path'

---

1. You will find no sign posts bearing this name or any sign posts marking this trail at all, although Murphy's Lane or the Blue Path have served as the name of this short trail in the past.

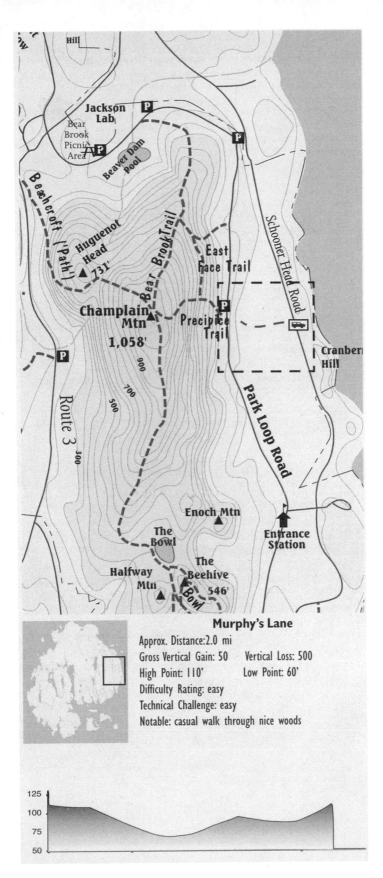

Murphy's Lane

Approx. Distance: 2.0 mi
Gross Vertical Gain: 50   Vertical Loss: 500
High Point: 110'   Low Point: 60'
Difficulty Rating: easy
Technical Challenge: easy
Notable: casual walk through nice woods

II. Region Two - The Ocean Drive Region

There are many coastal hikes in this region, several bordering one of the park's most popular area, Ocean Drive. Four hikes start from the Sand Beach parking area, while a fifth, the Ocean Drive Trail, extends to it, but easier access exists at the Otter Point parking area. Ability levels vary from easy to difficult, but most hikes in this region are actually moderate. Also included in this region is the longest single ridge on the island, Cadillac's South Ridge, extending 4.4 miles in its entirety.

Hike	Name	Parking	Level
2-1	The Great Head	Sand Beach	moderate
2-3	The Beehive	Sand Beach	difficult
2-5	The Bowl & Champlain	Sand Beach	moderate
2-7	Gorham Mountain	Sand Beach*	moderate
2-9	Ocean Drive Trail	Otter Point	easy
2-11	Hunter's Brook Trails	loop road etc.	moderate
2-13	Day Mountain	Rte 3 south of Blackwoods	moderate
2-15	Cadillac South Ridge	Rte 3 @ Blackwoods	moderate +

*Gorham Mountain has its own trail head, but starting this hike at Sand Beach allows hikers to form a good loop and warm up along the scenic Ocean Drive Trail.

Directions to Parking

Sand Beach: on one-way section of loop road, just past the toll booth.

Otter Point Parking: On loop road, parking area in on the right, after passing Otter Cliffs. It is accessible also from Rte 3; follow 3 south from Bar Harbor for almost 4 miles; take a left of Otter Cliffs Road, right on loop road to Otter Point.

Hunters Brook Trail Parking: on loop road, after it serves away from coast (and ceases to be 'Ocean Drive,' just after it passes under granite bridge (upon which Rte 3 crosses overhead); a cedar post marks the trail and a small parking area.

Hunters Beach Trail Parking: first left off Rte 3 south after passing Blackwoods Campground; a large green sign prohibiting most vehicles marks the road; parking area is a quarter mile down the road on the left.

Day Mountain Parking: 1.3 miles south of Blackwoods Campground entrance along Rte 3; parking for Day Mtn is in gravel lot on left, marked by a cedar post on right and a painted crosswalk in the road.

Cadillac South Ridge: diagonally across Rte 3 from Blackwoods Campground at a cedar post; parking is allowed on side of road.

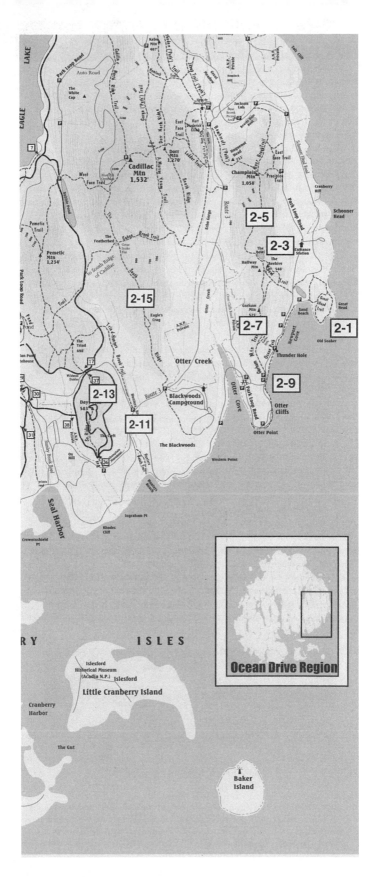

LAKE

EAGLE

Park Loop Road

Auto Road

The White Cap

Keba Mtn 407'

Jackson Lab.

A.N.P. Private

Eliot Cliff

A.N.P. Private

Hemlock Hill

Bear Brook Picnic Area

Dorr Mtn 1,270'

East Face Trail

Kurt Diederich's Climb

Beachcroft (Path) Trail

Huguenot Head 731'

East Gorge Trail

Cadillac Mtn 1,532'

Champlain Mtn 1,058'

Precipice Trail

Cranberry Hill

Schooner Head Road

West Face Trail

Pemetic Trail

The Featherbed

Cadillac Brook Trail

Gorge Trail

Route 3

2-5

2-3

The Bowl

Entrance Station

Schooner Head

Pemetic Mtn 1,234'

To South Ridge of Cadillac

Great Snake Flat

Halfway Mtn

The Beehive 540'

Sand Beach

Great Head Trail

Great Head

2-15

Eagle's Crag

Gorham Mtn 525'

2-7

Newport Cove

Old Soaker

2-1

The Triad 698'

A.N.P. Private

Otter Creek

Ocean Trail

Thunder Hole

17

Otter Creek

Park Loop Road

2-9

30

37

2-13

Route 3

Blackwoods Campground

Otter Cove

Otter Cliffs

Day 583'

38

The Croft

2-11

The Blackwoods

Otter Point

31

Ox Hill

Western Point

36

Ingraham Pt

Seal Harbor

Rhodes Cliff

Crowninshield Pt

RY

I S L E S

Islesford Historical Museum (Acadia N.P.)

Islesford

Little Cranberry Island

Cranberry Harbor

The Gut

Baker Island

Ocean Drive Region

The network of trails running over Great Head provide a good area for restless beach-goers to explore. These trails, along with some unmarked trails nearby, represent my first experience on Acadia's trails back in 1987. The land mass of Great Head forms the western side of Newport Cove, the inlet that houses Sand Beach. With the possible exception of Gorham Mountain, I traverse these trails more than any other.

The hike starts at the eastern end of the beach (furthest away from the parking area). A weathered cedar post marks the trail that rises along granite stairs into the hill side. At the unmarked, grassy intersection follow the trail to the right. It climbs over the layers of smooth rock left there by glaciers; blue paint and occasional cairns mark the trail. The beach and its inhabitants shrink quickly. Those who have no intention of making a full blown hike out of this will enjoy the view from the low height that gives a new perspective to Sand Beach.

The trail runs along the highest contour of the western side of Great Head, offering views of the beach, Ocean Drive, and points south. The rounds the point near where a radio station once stood, then begins the climb to Great Head, leaving the hubbub of the beach and Ocean Drive behind. The trail cuts away from the shore and swerves over rocky ground while rising and falling. Many quiet areas for picnic lunches or sunbathing provide alternatives to the beach.

Acadia's Schoodic Peninsula lies about eight miles due east across the bay. Lobstermen actively fish the deep waters around Great Head. Pleasure boaters, whale watchers, and guided tours pass the area at regular intervals. Rock climbers use the cliffs near the shore, although the trail shies away from the shoreline. Grassy areas abound for those seeking peace and quiet but don't want to lay on rocks. The trail continues to roll to its highest point, 145 feet over the sea.[1]

From this promontory, Schooner Head and the old Anemone Caves area of Acadia appear in the first cove on the shore to the north. Waves crashing on the shore sound distant from the height. The trail cuts down to the left but continues to roughly parallel the shore along the cove. The birch-filled section of trail that follows is among the system's most scenic. Bog walks and stone stairs fill the trail as it drops.

Cedar posts mark both left turns back to Sand Beach. The first trail cuts steeply back up the ridge that leads to Great Head and runs along its top edge, offering good views of both the Great Ridge of Champlain (including the Precipice, The Beehive and Gorham Mtn), and the Cadillac South Ridge behind Champlain. The next cedar post, located at the Schooner Head Road parking lot, marks a flat, well groomed path to the left. The trail heads straight towards Sand Beach roughly parallel to the brackish waters behind the beach's dunes. Salt air blows across the smooth, grass-lined trail with the sea breeze. The trail drops back to the beach just ahead.

Sand Beach from Great Head

---

1. During 1915, the Satterlee family who owned the area built the *Satterlee Tower* at Great Head's highest point. All supplies for this 18 foot diameter stone tower were carried to the top of Great Head by a donkey named Melba. It is estimated that Melba bore the burden of 35 tons of material (mostly cement and sand) for this tower that boasted a tea room, salon, & observatory.

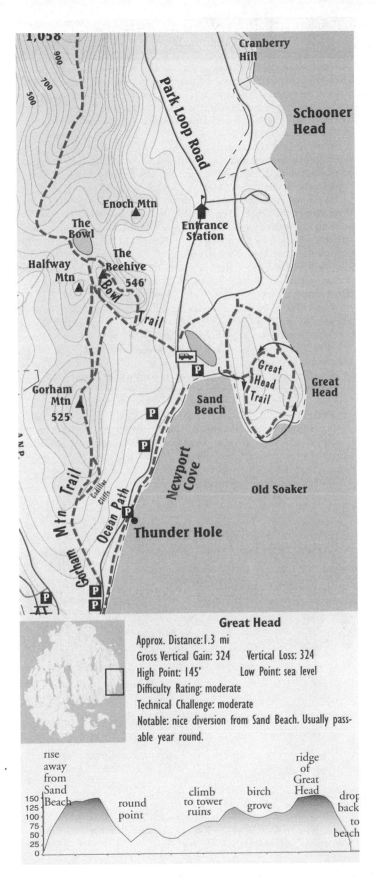

1,058'

900

700

500

Cranberry
Hill

**Schooner
Head**

Park Loop Road

Enoch Mtn

**Entrance
Station**

**The
Bowl**

**Halfway
Mtn**

**The
Beehive
546'**

Bowl

Trail

**Gorham
Mtn
525'**

Great
Head
Trail

**Great
Head**

P

P

**Sand
Beach**

P

Gorham Mtn Trail

A.N.P.

Cadillac Cliffs

Ocean Path

**Newport
Cove**

Old Soaker

P

Thunder Hole

P
P

P
P

Great Head

Approx. Distance: 1.3 mi

Gross Vertical Gain: 324   Vertical Loss: 324

High Point: 145'   Low Point: sea level

Difficulty Rating: moderate

Technical Challenge: moderate

Notable: nice diversion from Sand Beach. Usually pass-
able year round.

rise
away
from
Sand
Beach

round
point

climb
to tower
ruins

birch
grove

ridge
of
Great
Head

drop
back
to
beach

150
125
100
75
50
25
0

The Beehive juts up and out of the east side of the Champlain Mountain South Ridge. Its steep sides rise directly over the Sand Beach area. Similar in grade to the Precipice Trail on Champlain, The Beehive remains the ugly little brother to that trail, but because it was built by the same man who built the Champlain Precipice Trail, it originally bore part of the same name. Now simply "The Beehive" remains.

From the Sand Beach main parking area, walk to the right (against one-way traffic) on the loop road. The trail to The Beehive starts at a cedar post across the loop road, diagonally to the right from the Sand Beach lot. Odd shaped rocks fill the trail's first tenth of a mile.

At the first intersection, follow the trail to the right. The next sign warns of the dangers that lie ahead on the trail. The trail's steepest sections include iron rungs and ladders as well as an iron bridge.[1] The quick rise up the east side of The Beehive reveals a good view of Sand Beach and the swampy tributary that flows into the sea and extends to the north for miles. Good views of Acadia's Ocean Drive appear north to south. The iron rungs help climbers over the steepest areas, and rustic stone steps remain in place eighty-five years after having been set.

Prudent hiking and careful navigating will add to safe passage. The sheer side parallels the cliffs of the Precipice Trail that fades in and out of view to the north. Despite the steep grades, excellent footing over smooth rock as well as hard packed dirt and gravel provide measures of surety. No post marks the peak of The Beehive.

The hike continues to the left at the similarly unmarked intersection. As the trail drops, the village of Otter Creek appears between the long ridge of Champlain and the north end of Gorham Mountain (a nubble known as Half-way Mountain). A cedar post marks the next intersection and the hike continues to the left. After rounding the back side of The Bowl the trail reaches the intersection near The Beehive warning signs. The Sand Beach parking area lies a tenth of a mile down the trail and to the right.

NOTE: dogs should not be brought up The Beehive Trail.

The Beehive rises behind Sand Beach

1.A trail element that was borrowed from Prof. Brunnow's previous work on the now-abandoned section of *The Precipice Trail* that ran by the Great Cave; the book *Trails of History* traces the work of all path builders including Prof. Brunnow.

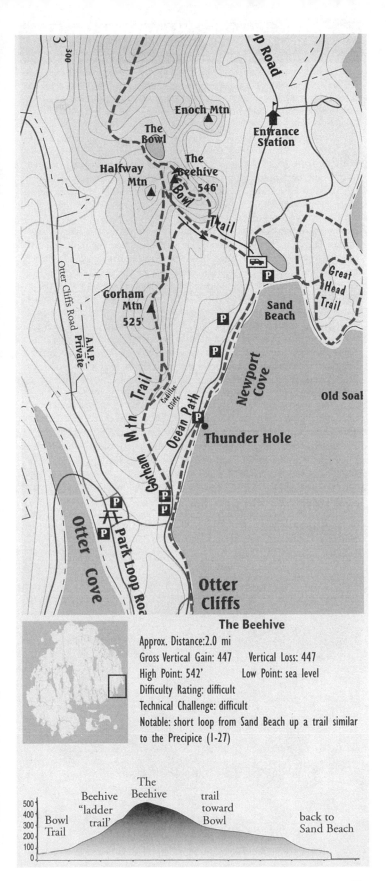

The Beehive

Approx. Distance: 2.0 mi

Gross Vertical Gain: 447   Vertical Loss: 447

High Point: 542'   Low Point: sea level

Difficulty Rating: difficult

Technical Challenge: difficult

Notable: short loop from Sand Beach up a trail similar to the Precipice (1-27)

The hike starts diagonally across the loop road from the Sand Beach parking area. As you exit the parking lot (on foot) take a right. A cedar post marks the start of the trail on the other side of the road. After a tenth of a mile of rock to rock walking the trail splits. Follow the trail to the left toward The Bowl.

Although fewer rocks lie in the trail, stepping stones provide the driest way to traverse the next section. Follow the trail straight ahead through the next two intersections. The trail reaches The Bowl at an intersection marked by three different cedar posts. Artist Frederick Church, a painter from the Hudson River School who was among the first to popularize hiking on the island., named this glacial cirque 'The Bowl.'

Near the water's edge, follow the trail to the left. Extensive bog walks provide dry hiking; beaver dams have raised The Bowl's level several feet over the last few years. At the next 'corner' of the pond follow the trail again to the left, crossing the small stream that flows from The Bowl. Smooth rock now provides the footing as the trail bends a bit more to the left before making a sweeping turn to the right. The first part of Champlain's South Ridge, visible from The Bowl, now faces you. This first stretch is probably the steepest portion of the hike.

The Bowl fades fast down to the right, and Sand Beach appears further away in the same direction. After rising over the next trail section much of the rest of the ridge appears, and ocean views improve dramatically. Occasional cairns and blue paint mark the trail as it curves higher. To the south Otter Cove appears along the loop road and Gorham Mtn, the southernmost part of Champlain's Great Ridge, appears further southeast. As I've mentioned in the Precipice Trail hike, I consider the ocean views from Champlain to be the finest on the island, and hiking Champlain by the South Ridge Trail offers a moderate alternative to the steep and strenuous Precipice Trail.

At 1,058 feet above sea level, no other peak on the island lies as close to the ocean at such a height. Most of the Ocean Drive coastline, as well as virtually all of Frenchman Bay, is in full view. To the west, Huguenot Head (see the Beachcroft Path hike 1-25) separates Champlain from Dorr Mtn. The top of Cadillac peaks above the top of Dorr, and the long South Ridge of Cadillac stretches over the village of Otter Creek to the southwest. Look to the south to return to Sand Beach. The 2.4 mile hike down provides excellent views along the entire route as it retraces its steps to Sand Beach.

The South Ridge of Champlain provides a backdrop to The Bowl

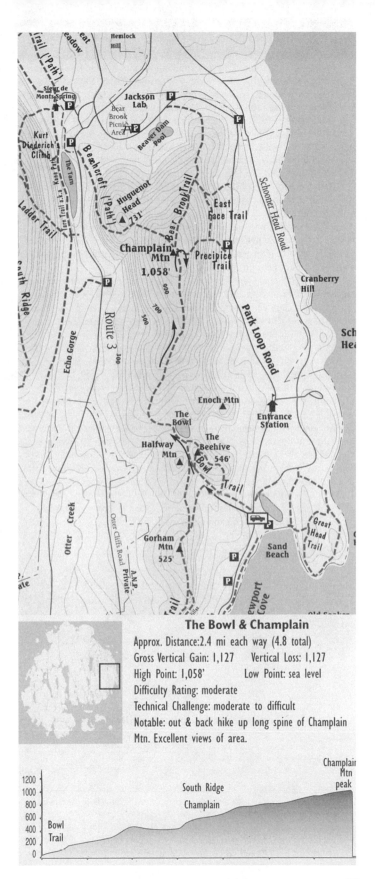

The Bowl & Champlain

Approx. Distance: 2.4 mi each way (4.8 total)

Gross Vertical Gain: 1,127   Vertical Loss: 1,127

High Point: 1,058'   Low Point: sea level

Difficulty Rating: moderate

Technical Challenge: moderate to difficult

Notable: out & back hike up long spine of Champlain Mtn. Excellent views of area.

Gorham Mountain makes up the southern reaches of Champlain's Great Ridge that rises along the eastern shore of Acadia. Gorham Mountain rises to its peak after a fairly easy one mile hike from the Ocean Path. I hike Gorham year-round, making 25-30 trips up the peak annually.

Great views, a relatively short hike, and nice loop constitute this route.

Hikers can park anywhere between Sand Beach and the Gorham Mountain parking area. I usually park at the upper Sand Beach lot and proceed down the Ocean Drive Trail southward to Gorham's trailhead (and parking area). The flat Ocean Drive Trail provides a nice warm-up.

From the back side of the Gorham parking area, a cedar post marks the trail's start over rounded smooth rocks. Cairns clearly mark the trail. At a signpost the trail splits.[1]

Since I usually run this trail, I almost always stay to the left, but the option to the right provides an interesting diversion, Cadillac Cliffs. This extended set of caverns was formerly a highly popular destination for fashionable hiking groups during the 1910s.[2]

The two trail spurs rejoin each other in about .2 miles and the trail rises steeply to the open stretch of Gorham's south ridge leading to the peak.

The top of Gorham appears another two-tenths of a mile up the trail. Sand Beach lies down to the east, bordered by the Great Head area.

To the south Otter Point, Otter Creek, and Otter Cove appear. Otter Cliffs lie along the eastern edge of Otter Point. The village of Otter Creek appears over the west side of Gorham, and The Beehive and Champlain appear to the north. Wave to your friends on the beach from the top.

From the signpost at the top, continue the loop by heading north by northeast. The path can be hard to follow at times as it drops toward the ocean, then around to the north ridge of Gorham. A good landmark is to bear to the right when the beach appears straight ahead. Cairns mark the trail as it heads toward The Beehive. Take a right at the first intersection, dropping through the woods to an intersection with The Bowl Trail. Stepping stones provide dry passage over the trail's wet sections as it cuts down the hillside.

Make another right turn on the Bowl Trail. The hike passes the steep Beehive Precipice Trail and continues straight ahead. It bends to the right where stones fill the final stretch. The trail empties onto the loop road directly across from the Sand Beach parking areas.

Gorham Mountain rises above Ocean Drive

---

1. A bronze memorial plaque to Waldron Bates, the father of Mount Desert Island's path system has been set here as well. Read about Bates' remarkable ground breaking works in the book *Trails of History*.

2. Another trail led to the Cadillac Cliffs from Ocean Drive. This trail lies abandoned today, and back then, Ocean Drive was a buckboard road. The CCC reformed the old Ocean Drive into what we know as the Ocean Drive Trail.

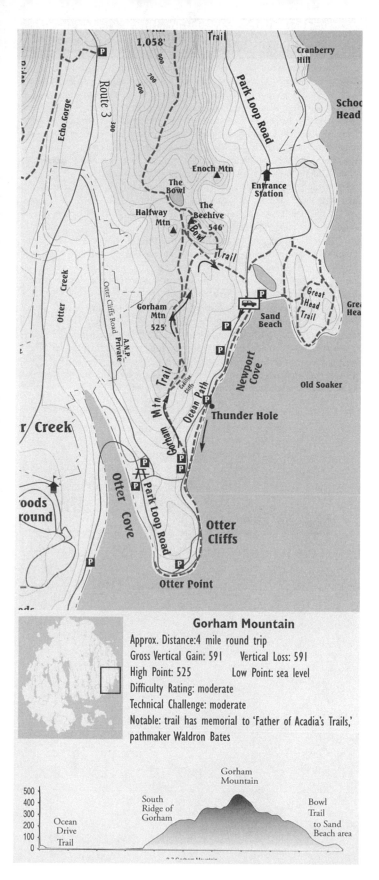

Ocean Drive stands as perhaps the biggest attraction to Acadia National Park. Of the millions that visit the island each season almost everybody makes it to Ocean Drive. From Sand Beach to Hunters Beach, the road attracts all sorts of sightseers. The park service provides a path that stretches from Sand Beach to Otter Point. The ANP trail crew has steadfastly restored Ocean Drive Trail[1] between 1996 and 2000, completely resurfacing the entire trailbed, and extending it past Otter Point. Built in the late 1890s, CCC crews first restored the trail in the 1930s. (The book *Trails of History* contains nearly 30 previously unpublished photos of the CCC's extensive restoration work.)

Parking areas lie along the right side of Ocean Drive between Sand Beach and Otter Point, and visitors can park in the right lane.

As the trail leaves the Sand Beach area, it drops to Thunder Hole, one of Acadia's most famous landmarks.

Baker Island appears to the south, while the far eastern edge of Little Cranberry Island peaks around the corner west of Baker's.

Ocean Drive Trail rises away from Thunder Hole, passing Monument Cove on the left. Next the trail passes the start of Gorham Mountain's south ridge, then proceeds toward Otter Cliffs.

The trail rises to the loop road where several car ads have been filmed in recent years (Acura, Chevy, Dodge, Ford) at the highest part of Otter Cliffs. I saw 32 consecutive full-moonrises from this point during the early 1990s.

The trail drops back toward the water, along a freshly restored surface. It passes a lookout at Otter Point, then curves northward as the trail runs toward the Fabbri picnic area. This terminus of the trail will extend toward Fabbri when construction is completed.

Ocean Drive

---

1. It may seem a subtle distinction, but the trail's proper name is *Ocean Drive Trail* rather than Ocean Path.

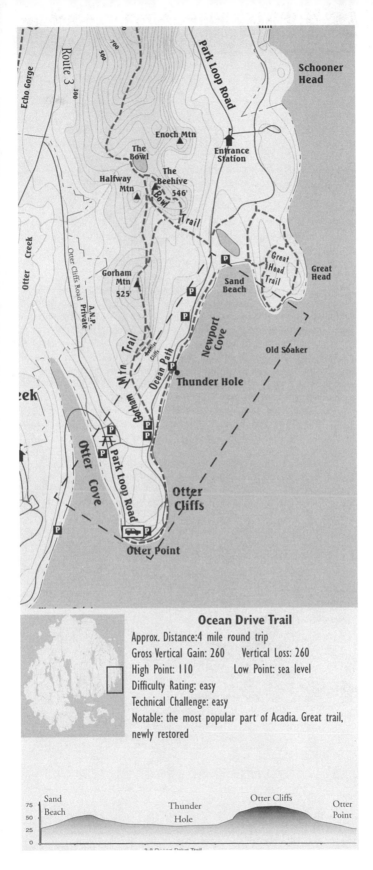

Ocean Drive Trail

Approx. Distance: 4 mile round trip

Gross Vertical Gain: 260   Vertical Loss: 260

High Point: 110   Low Point: sea level

Difficulty Rating: easy

Technical Challenge: easy

Notable: the most popular part of Acadia. Great trail, newly restored

As described here, the Hunters Brook hike goes point to point, starting on the loop road near where it heads away from the ocean, and ending at the Jordan Pond House. Hikers may choose to use the restaurant at the pond house as a lunch or snack spot before turning back. The one way trip covers about three miles.[1]

The trail cuts into the woods along the left side of Hunters Brook just after the granite bridge where Route 3 passes over the loop road. Hunters Brook represents to southern part of the watershed borne by the southwest side of Cadillac Mtn, southeast Pemetic, The Triad and Day Mtn. Beavers have dammed up several areas of Hunters Brook near the loop road.

The trail runs parallel to the loop road during its first 3/4mile, veering around the large pools formed by the beaver dams.

A mile later, the trail crosses to the left side of Hunters Brook and veers into the woods at the site of an old logging bridge, marked by remnants of a granite bridge.

After a short rise, the trail reaches the Bubble Pond carriage road and continues straight, but I recommend that hikers follow the carriage road to the right for about a quarter mile to the Pond Trail, the next trail that the carriage road crosses. The Pond Trail provides a far superior alternative to the continuation of what is now referred to by signs as "The Triad-Hunters Brook Trail." (Refer to the map if you'd like to proceed straight ahead.)

The Pond Trail cuts between The Triad, a tightly grouped trio of small peaks, and Pemetic Mtn. It crosses other trails in the area, but provides the best footing of any trail around. Its needle-covered floor and moderate inclines twist through a rich, lush forest. The great footing continues through cedar-filled forests as the Pond Trail drops to the loop road, crosses it, and reaches Jordan Pond. Take another left at the pond. A bridge of flat stones spans Jordan Pond (and the start of Stanley Brook on the left). Beyond the bridge the trail leads to the tea lawn and the pond house.

Appendage to Hunters Brook Trail: More hiking along Hunters Brook starts just off Route 3 just south of Blackwoods Campground. The first left after the campground (known as Sea Cliff Drive), marked by a green sign prohibiting buses, campers, and trailers, leads to a park trailhead to Hunters Beach. The parking area lies a quarter mile from route 3 on the left.

Other than the footing, the trail to Hunters Beach is easy; wet roots provide the biggest challenge. The half mile trail leads up to a little known cobble beach where the brook rumbles over the stones and Ocean Drive stretches off to the left.

The rocky Maine shoreline on display at Hunter's Beach

---

1. Hikers should plan to meet the driving members of their group after about two hours of hiking through the wonderful woods described in this hike.

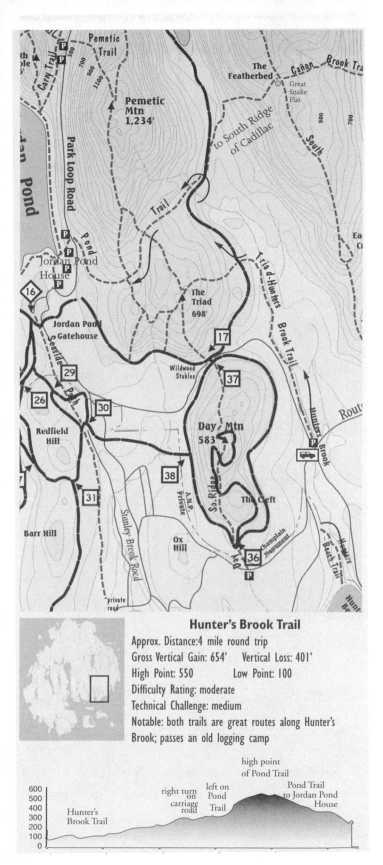

Hunter's Brook Trail

Approx. Distance: 4 mile round trip

Gross Vertical Gain: 654'   Vertical Loss: 401'

High Point: 550   Low Point: 100

Difficulty Rating: moderate

Technical Challenge: medium

Notable: both trails are great routes along Hunter's Brook; passes an old logging camp

As Route 3 twists and turns toward Seal Harbor from Otter Creek, it overlooks the Atlantic Ocean to the east. A cedar post marks the Day Mountain Trail and the Champlain Monument on the right side of the street (and a crosswalk extends to the parking area).[1]

Day Mtn receives its fair share of use, mostly by the Wildwood Stables carriage riders. Horses pull wagon-loads to the top where they can enjoy unobstructed views of the area around Seal Harbor. Short trails run up both sides of Day, and recent trail repairs have greatly improved hiking.

The trail starts from Route 3, rising for two-tenths of a mile over well-packed dirt before reaching carriage road intersection # 36. The trail to the top, marked by small cairns, starts to the left of the carriage road to the top. (Contrary to what other maps show.) The trail rises in choppy spurts. It tops clusters of massive boulders, flattens, and skirts rock groups again. In between, the trail crosses the carriage road three more times before reaching the top. Hikers should be grateful to avoid both the dust and the pasture patties generated by the carriage rides. Views abound from the top. The waters of Seal Harbor extend into the ocean and the coast of Maine. The village of Seal Harbor lies directly south of Day. To the east, the broad valley occupied by Hunters Brook separates Day from the South Ridge of Cadillac.

Pemetic Mtn rises to the north, and The Triad rises to the west. Although The Triad blocks direct exposure to the west from the top of Day, the sunsets from Day remain popular.[2] Wildwood Stables lies further west.

Two skinny sign posts mark trails that drop over the west side of Day. Skip the first one (the Wildwood Dane trail), but take the second option, a few granite blocks to the right of the first, known as the Triad Trail. It drops for four-tenths of a mile over a great example of the excellent repair jobs done by the ANP trail crew. Good footing through a well cut trail continues to the trail's end where the loop road crosses under the granite bridge (at carriage road intersection #37.

Follow the carriage road to the right. Few wagons, horses, or bikers use this section of carriage road. It runs basically along the contour of Day Mtn, offering easy walking or riding and plenty of great views of the ocean and parts of the Acadia coast. Overhead, the granite coping stones that line the carriage road appear between breaks in the trees. The carriage road passes by The Cleft, a cliff on this sheer side of Day Mountain.[3] The eastern exposure and proximity to the road make this part of Day Mtn ideal for watching the sun rise in total privacy. The left turn leading back to Route 3 (at intersection # 37) and the parking area lies about half a mile beyond The Cleft.

A zoom photo of the tiny island in Seal Harbor as seen from Day Mtn

---

1. The Champlain Monument was erected first in 1904 by the Hancock County Trustees of Public Reservations as a tribute to the explorer who "discovered" and named MDI.

2. Wildwood Stables has a sunset trip throughout the season.

3. Several seriously obscure lost trails once ran up to some caves located on the side of Day Mountain below these cliffs.

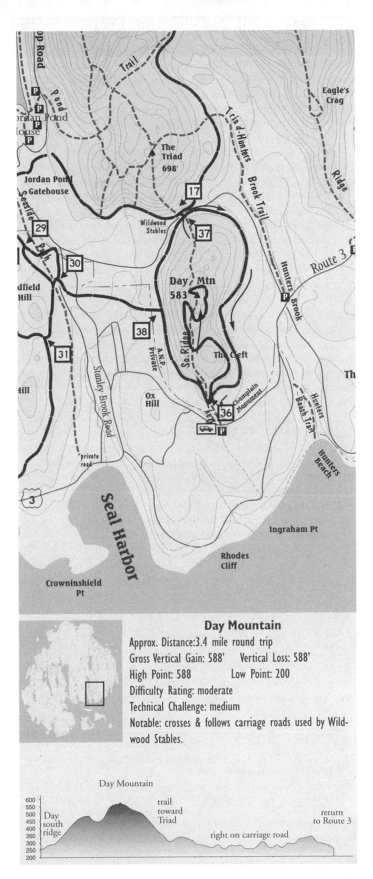

Day Mountain

Approx. Distance: 3.4 mile round trip

Gross Vertical Gain: 588'   Vertical Loss: 588'

High Point: 588   Low Point: 200

Difficulty Rating: moderate

Technical Challenge: medium

Notable: crosses & follows carriage roads used by Wildwood Stables.

Day Mountain

trail toward Triad

return to Route 3

right on carriage road

Day south ridge

When locals say they hiked 'The South Ridge' they refer to Cadillac's South Ridge. The trail runs 4.4 miles from the southern edge of Blackwoods Campground, but most hikers start near the entrance to Blackwoods on Route 3 from where the summit lies 3.7 miles away. The long, broad ridge affords spectacular views of the island's interior sections and the coastal areas.

A cedar post and granite stairs mark the most common start to this trail. The path winds over exposed roots between short stretches of soft dirt. It clears the thick woods, rises above the tree line, and meets a sign post in its first mile. The sign directs hikers toward Eagles Crag, a cleft that overlooks the Otter Creek area.

The South Ridge Trail continues straight ahead, and the Eagles Crag section rejoins the South Ridge Trail shortly. Both the west and the east faces of Cadillac drop steeply into broad valleys to the left and the right. Steep trails climb these sides,[1] but the South Ridge Trail provides a far more leisurely, sure-footed approach to the top. The trail winds through occasional small groves of firs and rises to the top of a knoll once called Dike's Peak.[2]

It next drops toward The Featherbed,[3] a small glacial pond (a cirque). The Canyon Brook Trail joins from the right and The Pond Trail (a.k.a. Featherbed Trail) rises from the left. The hike continues straight ahead. The short steep rise away from The Featherbed gives way to a long, gradual, wide open final mile. Pemetic rises directly to the west, while Dorr Mtn and Champlain Mtn rise to the east.

The furthest unlimited views available of the area continue as the trail nears the Blue Hill Overlook close to the auto road. Beyond this bend in the road the trail winds through a challenging stretch to the top. At the top rest rooms, snacks, and other amenities are available. For the return trip it is possible to avoid the hike's last awkward stretch by walking down the auto road to the Blue Hill Overlook parking area. The trail's long descent back to Blackwoods resumes across the street from the entrance to this parking area. The trail covers 3.7 miles back to Rte 3 and 4.4 miles to Ocean Drive.

The broad South Ridge of Cadillac stretches over the Atlantic Ocean

---

1. Several paths once made their ways up the sides of the south ridge; today only one trail climbs up each side.

2. When the United States Coast Survey mapped the island in the 1860s and 1870s, it had a station on the top of Cadillac (then Green Mountain). They coined many names for the area, especially around Dike's Peak. The names were often mythical in sort, and legends surrounded much of the area.

3. Formerly known as Great Snake Flat; see the book *Trails of History* for a thorough treatment of the legends of this area.

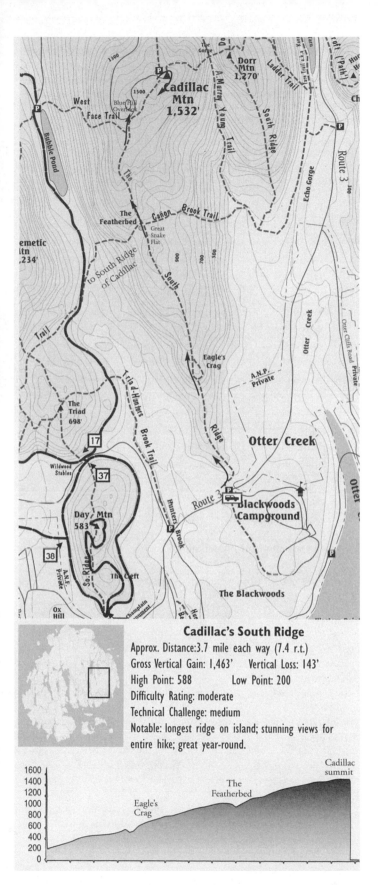

Cadillac
Mtn
1,532'

Dorr
Mtn
1,270'

West
Face Trail

Blue Hill
Overlook

The Gorge

A. Murray Young Trail

Ladder Trail

South Ridge

Route 3

Bubble Pond

The
Featherbed

Cañon Brook Trail

Great
Snake
Flat

Echo Gorge

emetic
tn
,234'

to South Ridge
of Cadillac

South

900

700

500

Otter Creek

Otter Cliffs Road Private

Trail

Eagle's
Crag

A.N.P.
Private

The
Triad
698'

Triad-Hunters

Brook Trail

Ridge

Otter Creek

17

Wildwood
Stables

37

Hunters Brook

Route 3

Blackwoods
Campground

Day Mtn
583

38

A.N.P.
Private

So. Ridge

The Cleft

Champlain
Monument

The Blackwoods

Ox
Hill

Cadillac's South Ridge

Approx. Distance: 3.7 mile each way (7.4 r.t.)

Gross Vertical Gain: 1,463'   Vertical Loss: 143'

High Point: 588   Low Point: 200

Difficulty Rating: moderate

Technical Challenge: medium

Notable: longest ridge on island; stunning views for
entire hike; great year-round.

Eagle's
Crag

The
Featherbed

Cadillac
summit

55

III. Region Three - Jordan Pond & Sargent Mountain Area

Among the island's most popular spots, the hikes in this region center around Jordan Pond. Although certain spots attract thousands daily, others remain quiet all the time. There are up to twelve ways to climb Sargent Mountain, the hub of most mountain hiking in this area and the island's second highest peak. This region offers some of the island's most challenging and rewarding hikes.

Hike	Name	Parking	Level
3-1	Conner's Nubble	Bubble Pond Parking	moderate
3-3	Cadillac West Face	Bubble Pond Parking	difficult
3-5	Pemetic Mtn East	Bubble Pond Parking	difficult
3-7	The Bubbles	Bubble Rock Parking	mod/difficult
3-9	The Triad	Jordan Pond Parking	moderate
3-11	Jordan Pond	Jordan Pond Parking	moderate
3-13	Deer Brook Trail	Jordan Pond Parking	difficult
3-15	Pemetic	Jordan Pond Parking	difficult
3-17	Penobscot & Sargent	Jordan Pond Parking	moderate +
3-19	Jordan Cliffs	Jordan Pond Parking	difficult
3-21	Seaside Path	Jordan Pond Parking	easy/moderate
3-23	Asticou Trail	Jordan Pond Parking	moderate
3-25	Sargent via Asticou	Jordan Pond Parking	moderate
3-27	Jordan Stream	Jordan Pond Parking	moderate
3-29	Little Harbor Brook	Rte 3; 1.3 mi. past Seal Hbr	moderate
3-31	Eliot Mtn	Rte 3; same as above	moderate
3-33	Asticou Terraces	Terraces parking area	moderate
3-35	Hadlock Ponds	Upper Hadlock Parking	moderate
3-37	Maple Spring Trail	Norumbega parking @198	difficult
3-39	Parkman & Bald	Norumbega parking @198	mod/difficult
3-41	Norumbega Mtn	Norumbega parking @198	difficult
3-43	Giant Slide	Rte 198 @ post	2nd most diff.

Bubble Pond Parking: on loop road between Eagle Lake & Jordan Pond

Bubble Rock Parking: on the loop road, just south of Bubble Pond parking

Jordan Pond Parking: at the pond house, overflow lots, and Pond Trail parking on loop road.

Little Harbor Brook Parking: 1.3 mi. past Seal Harbor beach; grassy lot just after small bridge

Asticou Terraces Parking: two-tenths of a mile before Asticou Inn on Rte 3 in N.E.Harbor

Hadlock Pond Parking: small gravel lot just north of 'Brown Mtn' Gate House on Rte 198; about one mile north of intersection with Rte 3.

Norumbega Parking: just north of Upper Hadlock Pond on the other side of Rte 198.

Giant Slide and Grandgent Trails: on Rte 198 at a cedar post, just past Sargent Drive intersection (also look for a sign for 'The old stone church').

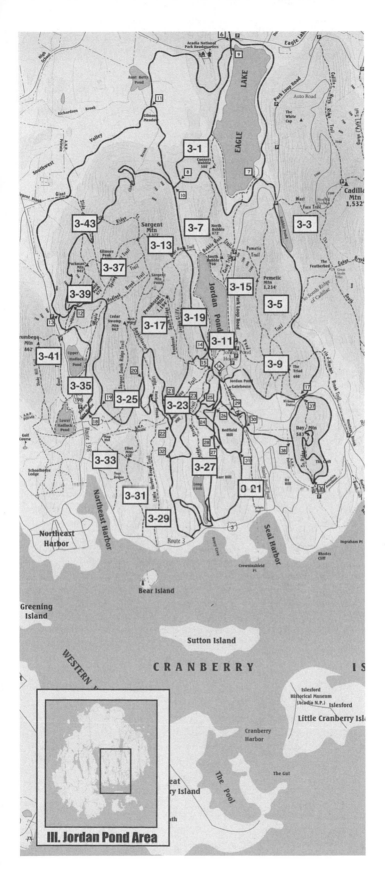

III. Jordan Pond Area

57

Many peaks on Mount Desert Island rise as mountains, extending north to south in ridges miles long, their tops looking over the island and the ocean for miles. Even the smaller peaks along the coast offer super views.

Conner's Nubble, located inland, rises to only 588 f.a.s.l., but offers excellent views of the area after an interesting hike. The hike covers ground through the woods, along a lake shore and to the top of the peak, ending along a carriage road.

Start at the Bubble Pond parking area, and cross the loop road. Follow the carriage road to the intersection (#7) with the loop around Eagle Lake. Take a left along the carriage road but watch for a signpost immediately on the carriage road's right side, marking the Eagle Lake Trail. Follow this trail to the shore of Eagle Lake.

Almost all of Eagle Lake's shoreline appears from the narrow, root-covered trail. Follow the trail to the left. The cliff-like side of Conner's Nubble appears ahead. The Eagle Lake Shore Trail has many rocks, slowing the pace of most hikers, but repair crews have improved the trail with boardwalks, and the hike remains high in quality. A signpost marks the shore trail's intersection with the Carry Trail that connects Eagle Lake with Jordan Pond.[2] Past this intersection small metal birds, stuck into the sides of trees, mark the trail above ground level, while blue paint splotches mark the trail's distance over the many rocks near the Eagle Lake shoreline.

A sign marks the trail up Conner's Nubble at the next intersection. If you reach the Eagle Lake carriage road you have journeyed a bit too far; backtrack about 15 yards to the Conner's Nubble Trail. The trail along the north spine of Conner's Nubble runs .4 mile over varied surfaces. Excellent views of Eagle Lake stretch to the north.

As you approach the top, the views broaden; Frenchman Bay appears further north, and a wide panorama of mountain views appear. Nearly every inch of Eagle Lake's shore appears from the top, including the swampy southern end where the hike began. Although only one-third the height of Cadillac, the top of the nubble seems to rise much higher. The top of Conner's Nubble is among many great spots to view peak foliage.

The nubble offers spectacular vistas. A panorama of views continues east with Cadillac and Pemetic, south toward The Triad, South and North Bubbles, and westward to Penobscot and Sargent. The flatness of the island extends inland to the west and northwest.

To descend, start from the cedar post and head toward Sargent Mtn (away from Eagle Lake). The trail drops in spurts over rocks before leveling. The back side of the nubble lies close to the carriage road (less than 1/4 mile from the peak). Take a left to return to the parking lot. The carriage road runs slightly more than a mile back to the starting point.

I usually ascend Conner's Nubble as part of a run around Eagle Lake, rising along the north ridge, and descending the way described in this hike.

---

1. Renamed Conner's Nubble after the CCC camp supervisor at MacFarland Hill during the 1930s; its original name was Burnt Bubble.

2. This trail is among the oldest paths on the island. Formed first by Native Americans then restored by the first generation of *rusticators*. See *Trails of History* for the complete story.

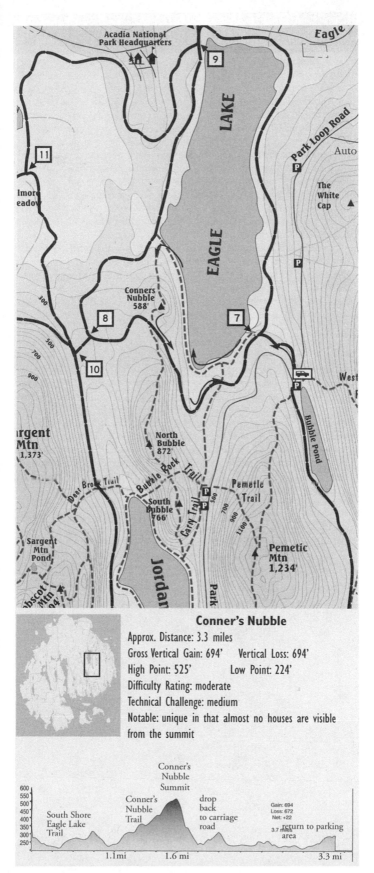

Conner's Nubble

Approx. Distance: 3.3 miles

Gross Vertical Gain: 694'   Vertical Loss: 694'

High Point: 525'   Low Point: 224'

Difficulty Rating: moderate

Technical Challenge: medium

Notable: unique in that almost no houses are visible from the summit

Of the eight ways to hike Cadillac, this is the shortest but most difficult route. From the parking area to the top of the mountain, the trail covers just 1.3 miles, scaling the vertical feet in a hurry.

From the Bubble Pond parking area walk to the north tip of the pond and follow the edge of the pond to the left. A cedar post marks the trail's start on the opposite side of the small foot bridge. Trees somehow have managed to cling to sections of the rocky start to the hike; metal diamonds in these trees mark the trail during this steep first quarter mile.

The trail runs along the contour of the mountain between uphill spurs. A prolonged push straight up completes a mile of hiking during which the elevation changes by 1100 feet. The trail meets the South Ridge Trail (see hike 2-15) at which point the upward climb has almost ended. Follow the trail to the left as it tops the final hundred vertical feet to the island's highest point at 1,532 feet above sea level.

Refreshments, rest rooms, and the widest views available anywhere on the east coast await on the top. The first mile of the return hike follows the South Ridge Trail for about a mile. The trail occupies a broad spine along the south ridge of Cadillac. Bubble Pond lies over the right side of the trail between Cadillac and the steep east side of Pemetic, which is visible from the trail.[1]

 It drops gradually until it nears The Featherbed, the small glacial pond (cirque) nestled into a bowl-like basin on the ridge. Near the Featherbed's edge the trail intersects with the Canyon Brook Trail (hike 1-23) on the left and the trail which drops back to Bubble Pond on the right.

Take a right, following the signs to Jordan Pond and Pemetic Mtn (along what I have labeled the Featherbed Trail). The first 200 yards of this trail are flat, but the trail drops more than 400 feet in the next two-tenths of a mile. Extensive restoration and rebuilding of this trail by the ANP trail crew includes stone steps, coping walls, and iron rungs and handrails.

The trail, marked by small metal birds stuck in trees, crosses a small stream as it levels and reaches an intersection with no signs. Follow the trail straight ahead. Bogwalks provide dry footing over this swampy area. The trail runs slightly upward and bends to the left across another stream. The trail then levels.

The Bubble Pond carriage road runs parallel to the trail on the right. This trail reaches the Bubble Pond carriage road at a signpost marking the Pond Trail on the other side of the path. Follow the carriage road to the right. The carriage road leads to the side of Bubble Pond, running close to its edge all the way back to the parking lot.

---

1. George Dorr believed all trails found in this hike were once a part of a trail system developed by the Native American culture which formerly inhabited MDI.

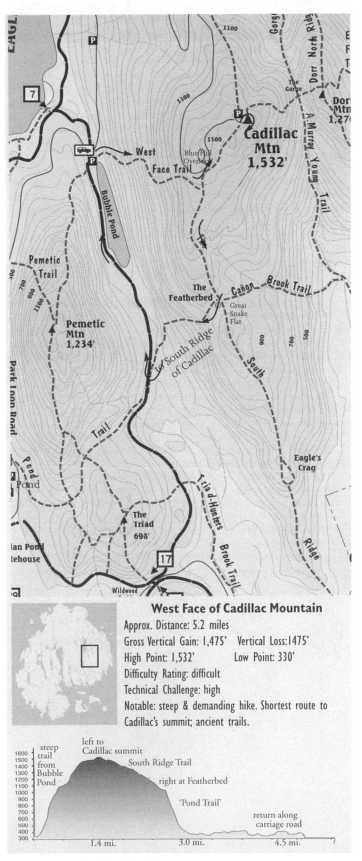

Map labels:
EAGL...
7
P
West Face Trail
Blue Hill Overlook
1100
Gorge
Dorr North Ridge
The Gorge
A. Murray Young Trail
Dorr Mtn 1,27...
E F T
1300
1500
Cadillac Mtn 1,532'
P
Bubble Pond
Pemetic Trail
Pemetic Mtn 1,234'
The Featherbed
Cañon Brook Trail
Great Snake Flat
South Ridge of Cadillac
South
Park loop Road
Pond
Pond
Trail
Eagle's Crag
Tria d-Hunters
The Triad 698'
Brook Trail
17
Ridge
lan Pond tehouse
Wildwood

West Face of Cadillac Mountain

Approx. Distance: 5.2 miles
Gross Vertical Gain: 1,475' Vertical Loss: 1475'
High Point: 1,532' Low Point: 330'
Difficulty Rating: difficult
Technical Challenge: high
Notable: steep & demanding hike. Shortest route to Cadillac's summit; ancient trails.

Elevation profile labels:
steep trail from Bubble Pond
left to Cadillac summit
South Ridge Trail
right at Featherbed
'Pond Trail'
return along carriage road
1600 1500 1400 1300 1200 1100 1000 900 800 700 600 500 400 300
1.4 mi. 3.0 mi. 4.5 mi.

The east side and the west side of Pemetic Mountain differ greatly. This hike describes the rise and fall along the eastern side of Pemetic Mtn. Starting from the parking area at Bubble Pond, walk down to the waters's edge.

Follow the narrow path to the right along the shore of the pond. A cedar post marks the trail up the northeast side of Pemetic after only about 75 yards along this path. The trail crosses a carriage road before ascending into the woods. Fir trees abound, and their needles cover the ground between a scattering of medium and small sized rocks. The lower branches of the pines, barren of needles, allow good visibility within the wood.

Within half a mile the trail starts to rise over a fairly steep grade. The zigzag pattern lessens the strain of the incline. Sporadic cairns mark the trail along with blue metal diamonds stuck into trees at eye level. Brown pine needles cover the trail making the surface slippery especially as it passes over smooth rock surfaces.

Intermittent views of Bubble Pond and Cadillac Mtn appear to the east as the trail passes in and out of forested stretches. The length of Bubble Pond appears to lie straight down from the trail, one thousand feet below. White stones line Bubble Pond's shore, while its floors drop steeply and the water appears dark blue.

The trail meanders along the east ridge of Pemetic. The sensation of walking directly over the water of the pond continues. Low bush blueberries line either side of the narrow trail as it rises, falls, and resumes its rise toward the top. Strangely, Pemetic appears to have two tops, separated by another drop. To the naked eye, neither peak appears higher than the other. However, a cedar post marks the high point on the southerly knoll which overlooks Jordan Pond, Penobscot & Sargent Mtns, and the Bubbles, all to the west.

The trail down the south ridge of Pemetic offers many outstanding views (some of the best, of Frenchman Bay & the Atlantic, in my opinion). The steep, rocky, sun bleached west side of Cadillac parallels Pemetic to the east. The gentle curve of the earth appears on the horizon over the ocean. Seal Harbor and the Cranberry Isles lie to the south. The long, bald south ridge of Pemetic reaches the tree line at a signpost.

Follow the Pemetic Trail that branches left toward the Triad. The trail nose-dives rock to rock over a particularly challenging stretch. Rock to rock hiking follows the steep drops. The trail reaches an intersection with the Pond Trail after a short flat section.

Follow the trail to the left toward the South Ridge Trail of Cadillac. When the trail reaches the carriage road, take a left on the carriage road. After a mile of gradual downhill, the carriage road reaches Bubble Pond. The parking area lies about .75 mi ahead.

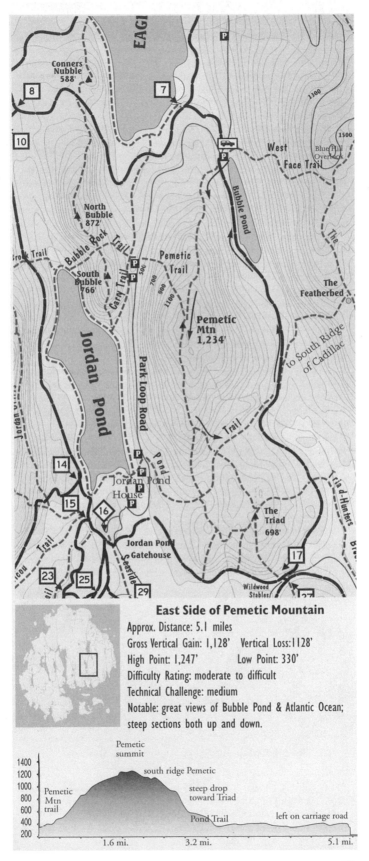

EAGLE

Conners
Nubble
588'

8

7

10

1300

1500

West
Face Trail

Blue Hill
Overlook

North
Bubble
872'

Bubble Rock Trail

Brook Trail

500

Pemetic
Trail

Bubble Pond

The

South
Bubble
766'

Carry Trail

700

900

The
Featherbed

1100

Jordan Pond

Pemetic
Mtn
1,234'

to South Ridge
of Cadillac

Park Loop Road

Pond

Trail

Triad-Hunters Brook

14

Jordan Pond
House

15

16

Trail

The
Triad
698'

17

ou Trail

23

25

Jordan Pond
Gatehouse

Seaside

29

Wildwood
Stables

27

East Side of Pemetic Mountain

Approx. Distance: 5.1 miles

Gross Vertical Gain: 1,128'   Vertical Loss:1128'

High Point: 1,247'   Low Point: 330'

Difficulty Rating: moderate to difficult

Technical Challenge: medium

Notable: great views of Bubble Pond & Atlantic Ocean;
steep sections both up and down.

Pemetic
summit

south ridge Pemetic

steep drop
toward Triad

1400
1200
1000
800
600
400
200

Pemetic
Mtn
trail

Pond Trail

left on carriage road

1.6 mi.   3.2 mi.   5.1 mi.

The Bubbles rise between Mount Desert Island's two most popular inland waters, Eagle Lake and Jordan Pond. Broad views overlooking these waters, the ocean to the south, and Frenchman Bay to the north. From the Bubble Rock parking area, hikers can choose between two ways to the top of South Bubble, home of Bubble Rock. Both start from the cedar post in the middle of the parking area.

One hundred yards from the parking area, you will reach an intersection. The highly popular trail to Bubble Rock goes straight and represents a short and moderately easy hike to the top. The trail continues over extensive crib boxes. At the next intersection, Bubble Rock and South Bubble lies to the left, while North Bubble's peak lies to the right. If you go left you will reach another intersection. From here, hikers could take a trail straight ahead, down a relatively steep trail to Jordan Pond. South Bubble is to the left.

Back at the first intersection, there exists an alternative route to the top of South Bubble. Take a left onto the Jordan Pond Carry Trail.

The Carry Trail's rocky surface drops down to the edge of Jordan Pond. From the pond's edge, take a sharp right to get to the top of South Bubble. The next stretch of trail will challenge even the most conditioned hikers.[1]

The trail proceeds rock to rock over very steep terrain. Great views of the pond appear immediately. Further south, vistas of the ocean appear. A few iron rungs help you over the steepest areas near the top of South Bubble.

The hike continues over the top of South Bubble towards North Bubble, now visible to the northwest. The trail drops to a signpost (mentioned earlier). Bear to the right at this intersection.

A left at the next intersection ferries hikers over new stone stairs as it rises steeply to the top of North Bubble. The height of North Bubble (872') offers panoramic views of the surrounding area.

Continuing to the north, the trail runs along the long north spine of North Bubble, offering superb views of Conner's Nubble, Eagle Lake, and Frenchman Bay. Both the east and west faces of North Bubble drop steeply to the left and right. The trail falls into the woods but levels considerably before reaching the Eagle Lake carriage road.

Here, hikers can pick up the Conner's Nubble Hike straight ahead (see hike 3-1) or follow the carriage road to the right. The carriage road intersects with the Jordan Pond Carry Trail after about a half mile. Take a right over the small footbridge.

This trail's pleasantries have lately been much improved by trail crews. Bogwalks help keep your feet dry while the trail rises during the next three-quarters of a mile. Hikers now return to the first intersection of this route. The Bubble Rock parking area lies just down the trail to the left.

Bubble Rock juts from the side of South Bubble.

---

1. Abandoned and no longer usable, the South Bubble Cliff Trail, built by the Seal Harbor Village Improvement Society, was this trail building agency's equivalent of Bar Harbor's Precipice Trail. This trail had iron rungs, ladders, and bridges along its sheer, cliff-side route. The book *Trails of History* traces the stylistic development of all island trails.

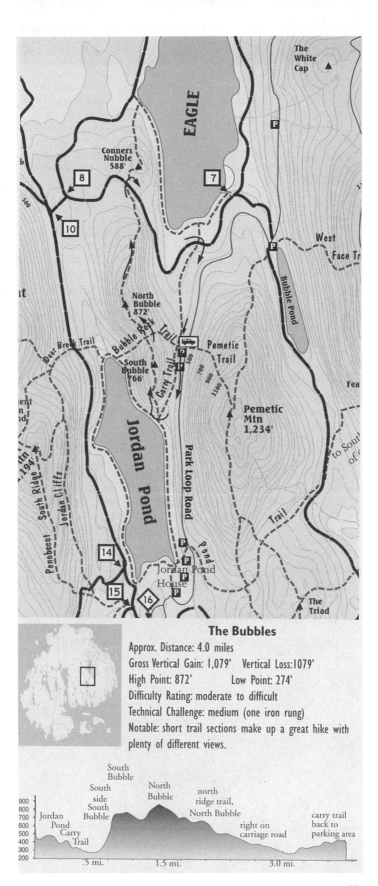

The Bubbles

Approx. Distance: 4.0 miles

Gross Vertical Gain: 1,079'   Vertical Loss:1079'

High Point: 872'   Low Point: 274'

Difficulty Rating: moderate to difficult

Technical Challenge: medium (one iron rung)

Notable: short trail sections make up a great hike with plenty of different views.

The Triad consists of three small peaks, with trails criss-crossing the woods offering access to two of them. Each trail has its own subtleties and covers varied terrain, but overall the trails appear similar. The Triad trails offer a quiet escape from the hubbub of activity around Jordan Pond House.

The best place to start this hike is from the small parking lot just north of the pond house on the same side of the loop road as Jordan Pond. (The trail is also accessible from any of the Jordan Pond parking areas. Walk to the edge of the pond and follow the Jordan Pond Trail to the right until you reach the bridge made out of flat stones. Just after the bridge, the signs mark the Pond Trail which rises to the large wooded area occupied by The Triad and Pemetic Mtn. Follow the Pond Trail across the loop road and Pond Trail parking area discussed above.)

Thick foliage encloses the trail as it rises away from the loop road. The first turn off the trail, a left, heads up Pemetic Mtn's Western Cliffs Trail. Yards later, the Pond Trail reaches a post marking a right turn to the Triad (.6 mile) at a small foot bridge. Follow this right. The trail rises then falls for a short stretch. Dead falls clutter the woods in this area. At the next trail intersection, take a left. (The trail to the right leads to a carriage road.)

Several stairs help the trail skirt up the side of some particularly large boulders, after which smooth rock dominates the footing.[1] Glimpses of Seal Harbor as the trail dips in and out of the woods. The trail rises and falls as it cuts a narrow path.

At the next sign post (a confusing intersection with six signs and two separate crossroads), you'll want to take another left turn, but take note of the following diversion: by taking a right at this intersection you can reach the highest of the three Triad peaks.[2]

Views from the small, bald top include Day Mtn to the southeast, and the waters of Seal Harbor to the south. Pemetic and Cadillac rise to the north. Retrace that tenth of a mile back to the weird intersection to continue this woodland hike.

The trail drops through the woods over a surface containing soft needles and exposes roots. It winds downward and reaches the Pond Trail once again. (hike 3-5 comes down the rugged trail across the Pond Trail from this intersection.) The course continues down to the left. The Pond Trail itself drops into a low, marshy area where several small cedar bogwalks provide dry passage. It rises back over some exposed roots to the first trail intersection at the Pemetic Mtn Western Cliffs Trail, but the trail smooths as it drops back to Jordan Pond.

---

1. The stairs bring to mind the style of Waldron Bates, father of Acadia's trail system, who served as a consultant to the Seal Harbor VIS as their path builders were just starting out. Bates' craftsmanship can still be seen across the island, and is fully documented in the book *Trails of History.*

2. Just over the right side of rock near this sign post you may find a plaque with the words "Van Santvoord Trail," a name given to this path in honor of a former Seal Harbor VIS path committee chairman.

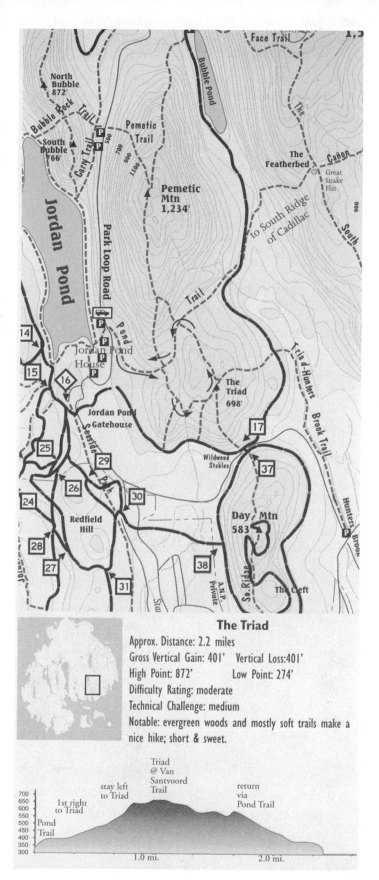

The Triad

Approx. Distance: 2.2 miles
Gross Vertical Gain: 401'   Vertical Loss: 401'
High Point: 872'   Low Point: 274'
Difficulty Rating: moderate
Technical Challenge: medium
Notable: evergreen woods and mostly soft trails make a nice hike; short & sweet.

67

The Jordan Pond House area serves as a hub for all sorts of carriage roads and hiking trails that snake their ways over the island. Carriages, bikes, and feet carry tourists in all directions from the pond house, and hikers of all abilities find pleasing trails to walk and climb. One trail that anyone can enjoy circles Jordan Pond.

The ANP trail crew began a major reconstruction of the trail along the east side of Jordan Pond in 1998. Their work has resulted in a wider, flatter trail. The trail receives huge use near the tea lawn, but crowds dwindle a bit further away. For almost its entire length the trail hugs the water, separated at most by a single row of birches on its east side, or by a row of firs along its west side.

Start by heading around the pond to the right from any of the parking areas. The trail runs along the southeast corner of the pond where the waters of the pond lap at the shore and the tops of the various large rocks that peak above the water line. The trail crosses Jordan Pond's outlet to Stanley Brook over a bridge of flat stones.

Many stream run off Pemetic Mtn's steep west side. This steep drop-off continues below the water line; Jordan Pond reaches depths of more than 100 feet close to the shore.

Across the water the rocky side of Penobscot Mtn hulks over the water. The Jordan Cliffs Trail runs along the steep face of Penobscot.[1] Trail crews plan to extend the restored surface around the entire east side. After a footbridge, the trail reaches the Jordan Pond Carry Trail and the South Bubble Trail. The Jordan Pond Trail's rocky surface continues into the north cove of the pond and passes another trail up to the Bubbles before reaching the valley known as the Southwest Pass.

Past the birch suspension bridge and the Deer Brook Trail (see hike 3-13), the pond house fades from view as the trail turns the corner onto the west side. Penobscot and Sargent Mtns block all but mid-morning sun from the west side. Fir trees line both sides of the trail, and their roots complicate footing. The first stretch along the west side of Jordan Pond also includes erratic, rock to rock hiking along the pond's rocky edge.

Closer to the pond house, extensive bogwalks help hikers over more rough areas. Hikers can clearly see the benefits of these elevated bogwalks as native flora and fauna have resumed growing over the former trailbed. Again, the thick woods block the steep side of Penobscot from view. The steep western side of Pemetic now appears across the pond to the east. The trail along the east side appears among the trees.

The trail completes the loop at Jordan Stream and the tea lawn. From the balcony over the tea lawn, telescopes magnify much of the trail including that strange phenomenon, the birch suspension bridge.

100 years separate these photos of the Jordan Pond trail. One is from 1900, one was taken in May 2000. Which is which?

---

1. Now abandoned, the Goat Trail runs up the western side of Pemetic; it offered challenges similar to those found on the Jordan Cliffs Trail.

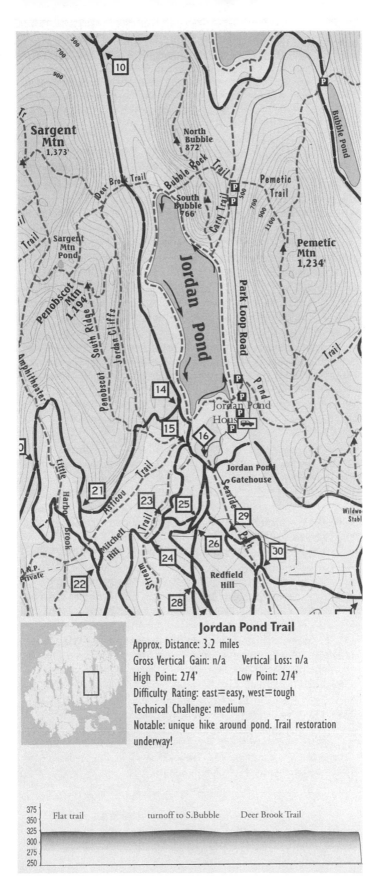

Jordan Pond Trail

Approx. Distance: 3.2 miles

Gross Vertical Gain: n/a   Vertical Loss: n/a

High Point: 274'   Low Point: 274'

Difficulty Rating: east=easy, west=tough

Technical Challenge: medium

Notable: unique hike around pond. Trail restoration underway!

The Deer Brook Trail represents one of the most challenging trails hikers can take up Sargent Mountain. I count the Grandgent Trail as the 'most difficult' trail up Sargent, but Deer Brook presents its own challenges. Built in 1917, the trail needs work, but it provides unique hiking terrain and views of Eagle Lake. As of 2000, the trail is closed for repairs but should reopen soon.

To create a good loop starting at the pond house, take the Jordan Pond Trail around the pond just as described in the first half of 3-11 (Jordan Pond Hike). Just past the birch bridge at the north end of the pond, the Deer Brook Trail begins, rising away from Jordan Pond over a rocky trail. The trail stays along the sides of Deer Brook for the next 1.3 miles.[1]

The trail crosses the "Around the Mountain" carriage road at the triple arched Deer Brook Bridge and continues to rise into the woods.

Rocky, steep, and eroded (and did I say steep?), the trail provides hard-core hiking, first passing an intersection with the Jordan Cliffs Trail (mild compared to this) and then the Sargent Mtn Pond Trail; stay to the right at both intersections, following signs toward Sargent.

After the second trail intersection the Deer Brook Trail starts up Sargent's northeast side (after having spent its first mile on Penobscot's east face). The Sargent Mtn section gets no easier. Steep, rock to rock hiking continues. Cutbacks lessen the strain over an otherwise extremely tough section. Eagle Lake stretches to the right as the trail finally reaches smooth rock. The top of Sargent appears suddenly as the trail cuts over the last of the steep sections and reaches the round top. Long, almost unlimited views appear in many directions.

The best way to return runs down the south ridge, duplicating the descent described in other area hikes. After just over a half-mile, take a left towards Sargent Mtn Pond at a sign post indicating this landmark. After dropping to the pond the trail rises away from it and rounds to the left, offering a good view of the back side of Penobscot Mtn (including the top).

The trail drops again, reaching a sign post nestled between two large rocks. Keep straight ahead, rising up to the top of Penobscot, and continue down its south ridge. The views from Penobscot's south ridge rival those of Sargent. To the east the steep Western Cliffs of Pemetic Mtn provide a backdrop to Jordan Pond. Marked by cairns the entire way (one could argue too many cairns) the trail remains scenic. It makes a sharp left turn just after the pond house disappears from view. Although blue paint marks this left, it can be confusing.

The trail from this point until the carriage road will remind you somewhat of the challenge of the Deer Brook Trail, dropping sharply to a carriage road. The cliff-side bridges help hikers, but everyone should exercise care on this steep, precipitous stretch.

You can return to the pond house via the carriage road by taking a left, and then a right at the first intersection, or by crossing the carriage road and dropping into the woods rock to rock. The trail rises to Jordan Stream and the pond house.

---

1. AYCC trail workers have done an exemplary job restoring stonework (c.1917) to its original condition close to the pond.

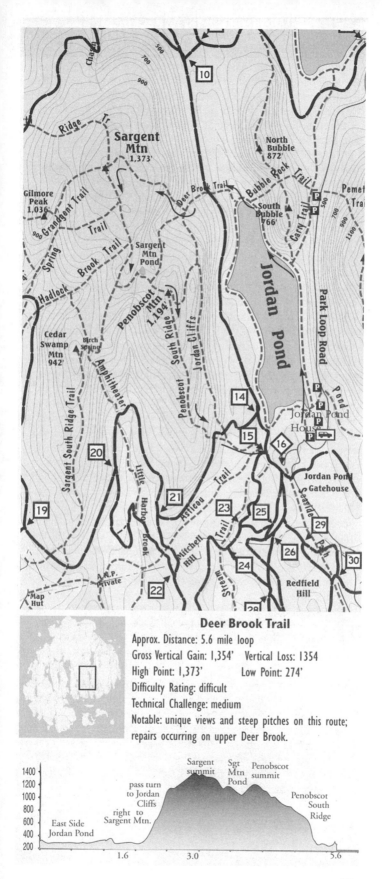

Deer Brook Trail

Approx. Distance: 5.6 mile loop

Gross Vertical Gain: 1,354'   Vertical Loss: 1354

High Point: 1,373'   Low Point: 274'

Difficulty Rating: difficult

Technical Challenge: medium

Notable: unique views and steep pitches on this route; repairs occurring on upper Deer Brook.

Pemetic Mountain occupies almost two miles of frontage along the loop road. Despite several sign posts marking trails up its sides, passing motorists can fail to notice the impressive mountain; most choose to look at Jordan Pond and the mountains on the other side of the road. As a result, Pemetic Mtn. remains obscure, uncrowded, and ideal for quiet hiking.

To start the hike, proceed to the eastern edge of Jordan Pond from any of the parking areas. Follow the shoreline trail to the right. Cross the flat stone man-made bridge, and pass the Pond Trail on the right, staying along the shore trail. (Although flat, the irregular footing and eroded surface along the pond can make the hiking tough.) About a mile past the stone bridge, a small wooden foot bridge just precedes the intersection with the Jordan Pond Carry Trail.

Follow this trail into the woods to the right. Pass the first sign post. The rocky and often wet Carry Trail reaches the wide, well travelled Bubble Rock Trail. Follow this trail to the right, crossing the parking lot and the loop road, and proceed into the woods up the Pemetic (Ravine) Trail marked by the cedar post. The trail proceeds rock to rock, rising steeply. Some cairns mark the trail, along with splotches of paint on both rocks and trees.

A brown pine post marks the small ravine along the left side of the trail. Hikers can hike either in the ravine itself or along the upper right side of it. The path in the ravine is actually a better choice. A wooden ladder climbs the back side of the ravine where another pine post marks the rejoining of the trails. The steep course continues ahead. A series of rock crib boxes provide passage along the final stretch before the trail clears the tree-line.

As with Acadia Mountain (hike 5-1). Pemetic Mtn boasts two peaks. After the intersection with a sign post, you will reach the first one. The second, however, is the higher of the two. From this peak the broad south ridge of the mountain appears. All of Jordan Pond appears with Jordan Cliffs providing a backdrop to the pond. The view from Pemetic gives the illusion of looking straight down into the water. The Cranberry Isles and beyond appear to the south.

Two trails run down the south ridge of Pemetic, and these two rejoin at a sign post lower on the ridge. Both reveal vistas of nearby mountains.

The trail along the eastern portion of the south ridge parallels sections of the Cadillac south ridge and offers great views of the Atlantic. The western section of Pemetic's south ridge showcases Jordan Pond.

The trails meet at a signpost where this hike proceeds to the right along the Western Cliffs Trail. Sharp drops characterize the next section of trail. An overlook offers a brief glimpse of the flat stone bridge that spans Jordan Pond near where the hike began. After passing the last of the rocky stretches the trail levels as it nears the Pond Trail. The hike continues to the right, presenting numerous pleasures over soft, needle covered earth. The trail crosses the loop road, drops again to Jordan Pond, and retraces the first stretch along the pond, returning to the Jordan Pond parking areas.

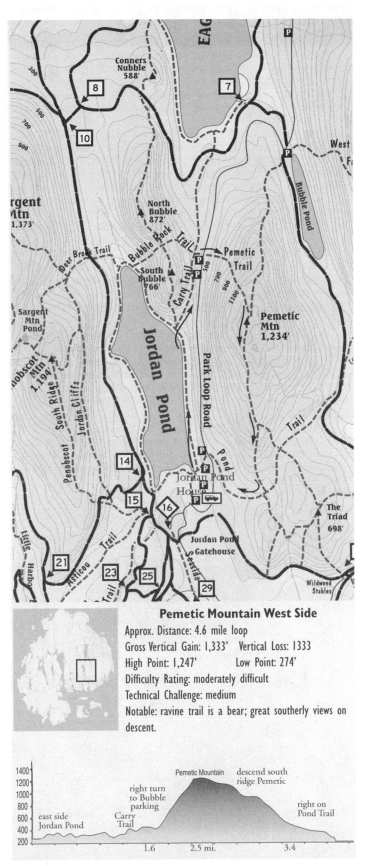

Pemetic Mountain West Side

Approx. Distance: 4.6 mile loop

Gross Vertical Gain: 1,333'   Vertical Loss: 1333

High Point: 1,247'   Low Point: 274'

Difficulty Rating: moderately difficult

Technical Challenge: medium

Notable: ravine trail is a bear; great southerly views on descent.

The Jordan Pond area is one of the most popular places on the island. Tourists literally swarm over the tea lawn during the peak season. Penobscot Mtn rises over Jordan Pond, and Sargent Mtn rises behind Penobscot to the north and west. The south ridges of these two mountains combine to give hikers the second longest ridge hike on the island. (Cadillac's South Ridge, hike 2-15, is the longest.)

The trail to Penobscot starts from the back side of the gift shop. A small sign marks the trail as it drops to Jordan Stream, crosses the foot bridge, and continues straight ahead. It drops down a rock trail then rises to the "Around the Mountain" carriage road loop. The Penobscot Mtn Trail starts on the other side of the carriage road with a bang: the first two-tenths of a mile of this trail represent the most difficult stretch of the entire hike. It rises steeply over rocks of all shapes and sizes. A hand rail and foot bridge assists hikers along the side of the mountain. The trail jerks upward again and cuts to the left over small, loose rocks until it reaches a flat, wide area of smooth rock.

From there, the trail makes a right turn and runs along the wide open south ridge of Penobscot Mtn. The top is visible the entire way, and superb views abound in all directions. Jordan Cliffs and Jordan Pond lie below, and the long Sargent Mtn south ridge lies to the west. The tops of Bald Peak, Parkman Mtn, and Gilmore Peak appear west of Sargent's south ridge from left to right.

The hike continues over the top of Penobscot and drops into the woods toward Sargent Mountain Pond as the trail curves slightly to the left.

Blue paint marks the Sargent Mtn Pond Trail. After a short, steep drop, continue straight at the trail intersection. The trail rises and runs along smooth rock. Penobscot appears to the left. The trail drops again and reaches the edge of Sargent Mtn Pond.[1] It continues ahead and rises steeply to the south ridge of Sargent Mtn.

At the next sign post follow the trail to the right. The half-mile hike to the top from this sign traverses mostly smooth rock, and rises moderately. Dome-shaped, only Cadillac rises higher than Sargent. But instead of a gift shop and a parking lot only a strong wind and an ever-growing pile of stones mark the top of Sargent.

A sign post with many signs marks the start of this hike
near Jordan Stream

---

1. During the 1860s, *The Lake of the Clouds*, as Sargent Mountain Pond was known, was at times thought to be both bottomless and the home to a mysterious serpent. One of these stories can still be proven false.

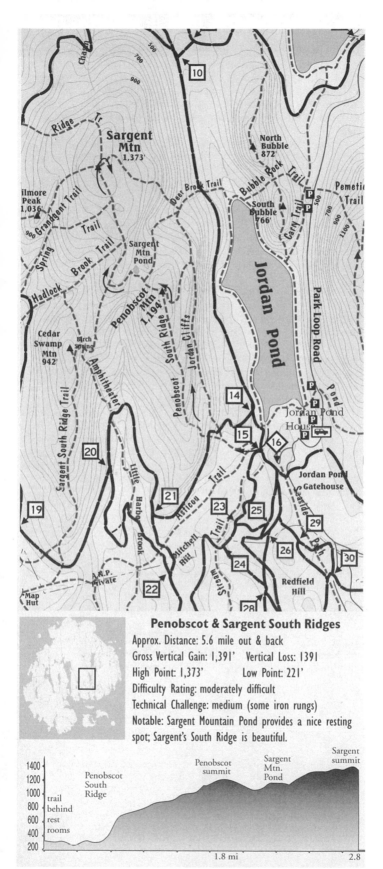

Penobscot & Sargent South Ridges

Approx. Distance: 5.6 mile out & back
Gross Vertical Gain: 1,391'   Vertical Loss: 1391
High Point: 1,373'   Low Point: 221'
Difficulty Rating: moderately difficult
Technical Challenge: medium (some iron rungs)
Notable: Sargent Mountain Pond provides a nice resting spot; Sargent's South Ridge is beautiful.

The frozen rock slide down the east side of Penobscot Mountain commands attention from the loop road along Jordan Pond. The large boulders form a messy pile emerging from water level and extending up to the 1,194 foot high peak. Amazingly, trail builders constructed a path that runs most of the length of the cliff, approximately halfway up. Obviously, it is a rocky path.

Waldron Bates (1856-1909), the island's most prolific path builder, built the island's first cliff-side trail before 1900 when he constructed the northern section of the trail, known as Jordan Bluffs.[1]

I often send visiting friends up this trail so they can enjoy its dramatic vistas, varied terrain, and unique aspects.

To access the southern section (known as Jordan Cliffs), follow the trail behind the rest rooms at Jordan Pond House toward Sargent and Penobscot Mountain trails. Cross the carriage road and foot bridge. Follow the cedar post's directions toward Penobscot and Sargent. The trail drops to the base of the ridge formed by Penobscot Mountain, then rises over several sets of stairs.[2]

A sign post marks the Jordan Cliffs Trail to the right just as the "Around the Mountain" carriage road appears above. A cedar post marks the Jordan Cliffs trail on the other side of the carriage road. Jordan Cliffs represents one of the island's most challenging (and dangerous) trails. Just up the trail, another sign warns hikers to exercise care. Stone steps, iron rungs, railings, and various bridges provide additional assistance. Hikers and climbers still must exercise caution and common sense on this trail.

Like the Precipice, the Jordan Cliffs Trail contains drops and flat sections along with the steep rises. A jagged, log-carved bridge spans one ravine. Views of Jordan Pond, the tea lawn, Pemetic Mountain and the Bubbles appear from the face of Jordan Cliffs.

As the trail bends around huge boulders, it intersects with the Deer Brook Trail. Continue along the Jordan Cliffs Trail to the left. Iron rungs and ladders assist hikers over this section, the Jordan Bluffs. Once clear of the iron, small cairns and blue paint mark the trail as it cuts back along the east face of Penobscot and crosses back into the South Ridge Trail.

Penobscot's summit lies up and to the right (shown incorrectly on other maps). The bald top of Penobscot offers super views in all directions. Hulking Sargent Mtn appears to the west, connected to Penobscot by the Sargent Mtn Pond Trail (see hike 3-17).

Return to the Jordan Pond parking area along Penobscot's South Ridge Trail. Vistas of the ocean, islands, and mountains in the area appear from this wide open ridge. The long south ridge of Sargent lies due west.

The trail makes a tricky left turn just after the tea house and the pond disappears from view. Blue paint and a cairn mark this left turn.

Another steep, technical stretch of trail drops to the carriage road near the start of the Jordan Cliffs Trail. Hikers can return to the parking area via the original first stretch of rocky trail straight ahead, or by taking a left on the carriage road, followed by a right to return to Jordan Pond.

---

1. Bates' original trail ran only part way up the northern section of this path. At the time, Jordan Bluffs and Jordan Cliffs were viewed as two separate entities.

2. Stairs such as these characterize virtually all intersections between carriage roads and roads, and reflect the concern John D.Rockefeller, Jr. had for the trails during the construction of the carriage roads. Since almost every trail preceded each carriage road, the stonework and additional coping that carriage road workers put in place illustrate one way that the carriage roads directly improved the trails of Acadia.

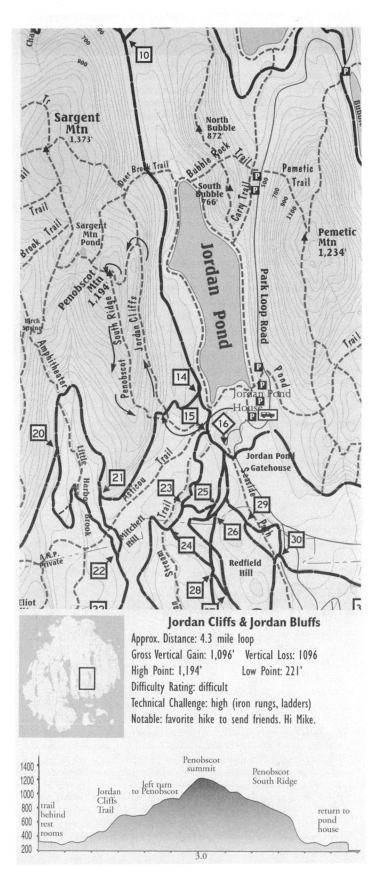

Jordan Cliffs & Jordan Bluffs

Approx. Distance: 4.3 mile loop

Gross Vertical Gain: 1,096'   Vertical Loss: 1096

High Point: 1,194'   Low Point: 221'

Difficulty Rating: difficult

Technical Challenge: high (iron rungs, ladders)

Notable: favorite hike to send friends. Hi Mike.

The Jordan Pond area retains high popularity at Acadia. Attractions include walking around the water, hiking up the nearby mountains, browsing in the gift shop, and eating at the restaurant.

A network of trails and carriage roads radiate from Jordan Pond. A handful of intensely popular trails attract most visitors. Others, like the Seaside Path, absent from many map editions, provide all the pleasures of the park without the crowds.[1]

To access the Seaside Path[2] start from the main parking area at Jordan Pond. A wood-chipped path, lighted by small lamps, runs across the front lawn near the small fenced flower garden. Follow this path until it meets the carriage road near the granite gate on the left and the Jordan Pond House worker's dorm ahead. Take a right on the carriage road, followed by an immediate left onto the trail. The only sign marking this trail lies ten feet off the start of the trail. Nailed to the side of a tree, about six feet up, the sign simply says "Seal Harbor."

Excellent footing covers the entire tree-lined trail. Blue paint splotches mark the trail's narrow passage through the woods. The horses will probably sense your presence as you pass by the stable and corral.

The trail crosses carriage roads several times just after the stables. Occasional signs denote the trail simply as "Seaside Trail." The trail drops a bit and passes over moss-covered stones and makes its first real bend. Rocks and high ground on the side of the trail provide dry passage over the wet areas.[3]

As the Seaside Path passes under the Stanley Brook bridge it enters private land.[4] While a carriage road converges from the right, the Stanley Brook section of the loop road nears from the left. Past the bridge excellent footing continues. The road and carriage road veer away from the quiet trail. After passing a stony, eroded section, the trail crosses a paved road, enters a mature fir grove, and ends at a well groomed gravel road.

The trail once connected the Seaside Inn with the Jordan Pond House area. The Seaside Inn, along with The Glencove, were two large Seal Harbor hotels of an earlier era. At different stages of development the path has served as a buckboard road.

On clear days the waters of Seal Harbor appear from the end of the Seaside Path. Nearby the sands of Seal Harbor beach and the lush lawn of the nearby village green provide ideal picnic spots. The picturesque beach provides a relaxing rest stop, and tidal patterns can warm the water in Seal Harbor into the sixties. Return to the parking area by following the Seaside Trail in the opposite direction, or connect to the pond house by following the appropriate carriage roads.

Seal Harbor, one endpoint of this hike

1. The Seaside path begins on park land. It passes onto private land past the Stanley Brook Bridge. Please respect the rights of the private property owners in this area.

2. If you look closely, a broken down old-style signpost still bears the words "Seaside Path" as it leads away from the Jordan Pond House main parking area; a fallen tree blocks clean passage to the 'start' of this path.

3. Just beyond this wet area, you may come across a bronze memorial plaque to Edward L. Rand, a former path committee chairman of the Seal Harbor VIS and an important figure in the development of MDI's paths and path maps. *Trails of History* discusses Rand's expertise and shows several photos of his brother Henry Rand, a prolific, renowned photographer.

4. The landowners have been gracious enough to offer public access across their land. Hikers are expected to respect the landowner's courtesies.

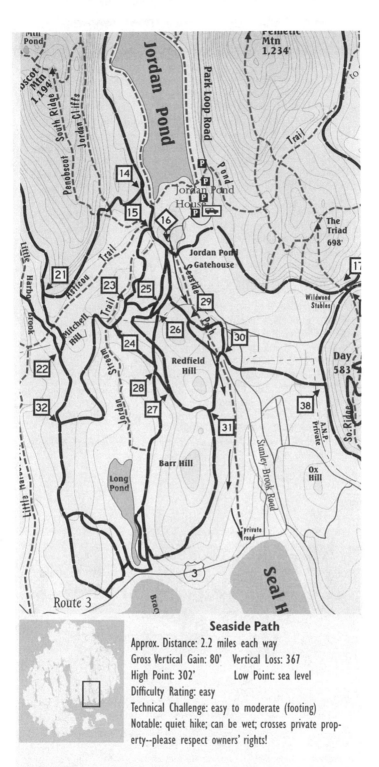

Seaside Path

Approx. Distance: 2.2 miles each way

Gross Vertical Gain: 80'   Vertical Loss: 367

High Point: 302'   Low Point: sea level

Difficulty Rating: easy

Technical Challenge: easy to moderate (footing)

Notable: quiet hike; can be wet; crosses private property--please respect owners' rights!

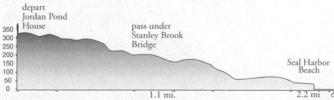

79

The Asticou Trail stands out as an excellent trail to hike. The surface remains well kept and the trail's width allows two-by-two hiking most of the way. The trail passes through interesting and beautiful woods, crossing several trails and carriage roads along its way.[1]

From the back of the pond house gift shop (by the rest rooms) enter the trail at the opening of the woods. Continue over the foot bridge straight ahead (not the carriage road bridge to the left) across Jordan Stream then bear left down the Asticou Trail. The trail runs its entire length without making any turns or breaks.[2] In the first 1.5 miles it rolls through quiet woods over soft pine needles. Stepping stones usually provide dry passage over wet areas.

After a brief rise the trail crosses a carriage road. The trail drops as it crosses another carriage road and continues to Little Harbor Brook. Cross the cedar bridge, continuing straight. (The left turn runs south along Little Harbor Brook.) This hike rises slowly away from the brook. You will need to work a bit as the pitch increases over a short rocky area, the only such area on this hike. Stairs hewn of natural granite help hikers over the steepest section.

After several granite steps, the trail bends as it rises past the Eliot Mtn turnoff to the left. Bear right here. The trail narrows through firs and passes Sargent's South Ridge Trail on the right. The trail reaches the Map Hut at the intersection of another trail up Eliot Mountain on the left. This hut provides a nice resting stop or a place to have a picnic.

Hikers must now decide whether to head back to the pond house or forge on over Eliot Mountain to the left.[3] I recommend going over Eliot.

The short hike over Eliot Mountain will bring you across the top of this small peak along a wooded trail that is closing in on itself. After passing the top, take lefts at both intersections and you will end up at the intersection you passed at the top of the granite stair flights.

Or you may choose to return to the pond house by retracing the Asticou trail, following it without making any turns.

The Asticou Azalea Gardens.

---

1. During the hey-day of MDI path building, the Asticou Trail served as a hub for no less than a dozen spur trails in the area; most are 'abandoned' today.

2. Believe it or not, a railroad was once proposed over this wide, quiet route.

3. When originally restored as a trail in the 1900s, the Asticou Trail was a joint effort of both the Seal Harbor and Northeast Harbor Village Improvement Societies. While the SH VIS worked from the pond house, the NEH VIS worked north from Asticou. The trail then served as a perfect example of the "island-wide system" espoused by the path makers of this era; it connected the Seal Harbor System to the Northeast Harbor System, and connected the ever-popular Jordan Pond House to Northeast Harbor as well. All hikers were free to pass down the gravel road to the Asticou Inn. Current landowners south of the map hut no longer see things this way and desire privacy. See the book *Trails of History* for the whole story.

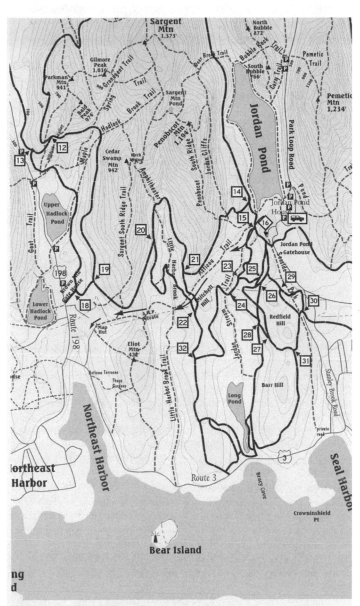

Asticou Trail

Approx. Distance: 2.3 miles each way

Gross Vertical Gain: 480'   Vertical Loss: 600'

High Point: 422'   Low Point: 48'

Difficulty Rating: easy

Technical Challenge: easy to moderate (footing)

Notable: crosses private property--please respect owners' rights! Gateway to arcane, scenic system.

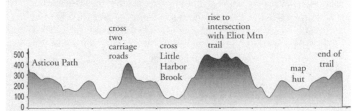

Sargent Mountain looms over the Somes Sound area on MDI's east side. The island's second highest peak, Sargent offers none of the hassles yet most of the views available from Cadillac, and its south ridge contains one of the longest trails on the island. Hikers have sensational views from start to finish along this woodland trail, and there is no auto road, no gift shop, and no tour buses!

The Asticou Trail begins at Jordan Stream just south of Jordan Pond. A sign directs hikers to the trail from behind the pond house, near the public rest rooms. Cross the foot bridge and follow the Asticou Trail to the left. The smooth, peaceful trail rolls basically downhill for 1.2 miles, crossing carriage roads twice. It crosses the Little Harbor Brook foot bridge and continues on the other side. The incline increases away from the bridge and passes the Eliot Mtn/Thuya Garden turnoff on the left. The narrow trail passes through a grove of small firs. A sign marks the Sargent Mountain South Ridge Trail on the right.

The mountain peak lies 2.1 miles from this sign. The trail rises to the 'Around the Mtn' carriage road loop, crosses it, and begins to rise along the Cedar Swamp Mtn section of Sargent's south ridge. You'll see tremendous vistas to the east over the valley formed by Sargent and Penobscot most of the way. Almost no turns or intersections exist to confuse or confound hikers, and cairns clearly mark the trail. The trail has short descents between long uphill stretches as it approaches Cedar Swamp Mtn's peak.

The trail drops into the sharp valley between Sargent and Penobscot before reaching Cedar Swamp's peak, however. If you make it to the sign marking the top of Cedar Swamp Mtn you have gone a bit too far; retrace your steps about 100 yards to regain the trail of this hike. The trail drops sharply to Birch Spring. From Birch Spring, the Amphitheater Trail drops to the right (hike 3-29), while the trail to the left leads to the rough & tumble Hadlock Brook Trail (hike 3-37) which also rises to the top of Sargent.

A sign directs you towards Sargent Mtn, 1.1 miles from Birch Spring. The trail rises steeply across an open ridge to the intersection with the Sargent Mtn Pond Trail. From there, it rises gradually over the bald, broad dome of Sargent Mtn. The top of Sargent offers superb views in all directions. Car mirrors and windshields glisten in the sun as they climb Cadillac's auto road to the east. Penobscot separates Sargent from Jordan Pond, but nothing stands in front of the views of the Gulf of Maine to the south.

Unlimited views stretch down the shore and out to sea. Somes Sound, the island's west side, and the mainland stretch to the west. To return go back to the Sargent Mtn Pond Trail. It drops steeply to the pond only to rise just as steeply away from it before climbing blindly to the top of Penobscot.

The views from Penobscot compare well to those from Sargent, and now Jordan Pond appears over the east face of Penobscot. The trail down the south ridge of Penobscot skirts its eastern extreme as well, peering over into Jordan Pond. The gradual descent allows hikers to view the island's south end easily. The pond house disappears from view as the trail levels and takes a sneaky but important left turn. After turning the trail drops steeply to the carriage road over rocky areas, assisted by railings and bridges provided by the park service. To return to Jordan Pond either follow the trail on the other side of the carriage road, or take a left down the carriage road, followed by a right.

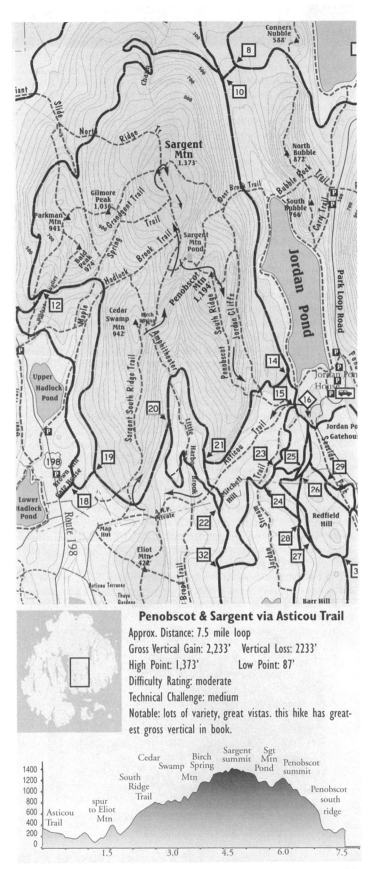

Penobscot & Sargent via Asticou Trail

Approx. Distance: 7.5 mile loop

Gross Vertical Gain: 2,233'   Vertical Loss: 2233'

High Point: 1,373'   Low Point: 87'

Difficulty Rating: moderate

Technical Challenge: medium

Notable: lots of variety, great vistas. this hike has greatest gross vertical in book.

Jordan Pond represents a large watershed, and Mount Desert Water Company draws much of its water supply from the pond. Mountain streams run into the pond from the Triad, Pemetic, North and South Bubble, and Penobscot, but only two streams run out of the pond. Jordan Stream constitutes the major part of the flow from the pond. In its dash (almost) to the sea, Jordan Stream evolves from youth to maturity. The stream terminates in the marshy north end of Seal Harbor's Long Pond.

A trail runs along the stream to the edge of the marsh. Most other maps fail to include parts or all of this trail. The trail then rises away from the stream and intersects with a private carriage road.

The trail gets high marks for its gradual grades, lack of crowds, terrain covered, unique aspects, and picnic potential. However, much of its treadway has been badly eroded. To reach this trail, walk down the short trail that starts behind the public rest rooms at Jordan Pond House.

A cedar post marks the Jordan Stream Trail on the left side (facing downhill). The trail travels down the left side of the stream over a series of flat rocks. It crosses the carriage road and continues down the other side of the gurgling stream. A canopy of foliage blocks most sunlight; like the Gorge Path (hike 1-19) the Jordan Stream Trail can stay cool even on the hottest summer days. Exposed roots and rocks can make hiking difficult.

Perhaps the most scenic aspect to this trail is the Cobble Bridge. Faced with cobbles rather than granite, this bridge is unique in the carriage road system. Jordan Stream Trail passes under the bridge and continues its course. South of the bridge, small, bouncy (but slippery-when-wet) foot bridges cross the stream repeatedly.

One such bridge contains a trail marker sign on the left side of the stream. Ignore this sign and this bridge!

The hike continues along the right side of Jordan Stream; marsh grass and a wider flood plain mark the coming of the marsh. The trail, still on the right side of the stream, rises a few feet and veers briefly to the right. When it returns to the water it crosses a bridge and leaves the water, cutting over the wet ground along a series of bogwalks.

Marsh grass grows tall on both sides of the walk, often obscuring it from view. The trail cuts over a web of exposed roots of large pines before it reaches a carriage road. The field to the right extends a mile to the sea, bordering little Long Pond, the outgrowth of the marsh formed by the stream's flow. A carriage road runs along it, and half a mile later another road, covered with grass, cuts off the gravel path to the right. It runs closer to Long Pond, passing the oft-photographed Long Pond boat house.

To the north the rocky ridges of Penobscot and Sargent rise. Beyond the boat house only Route 3 and a small sea wall separate Long Pond from the ocean. Return to the Jordan Pond area by the same route (or follow carriage roads back).

The scenic Cobble Bridge spanning the Jordan Stream Trail

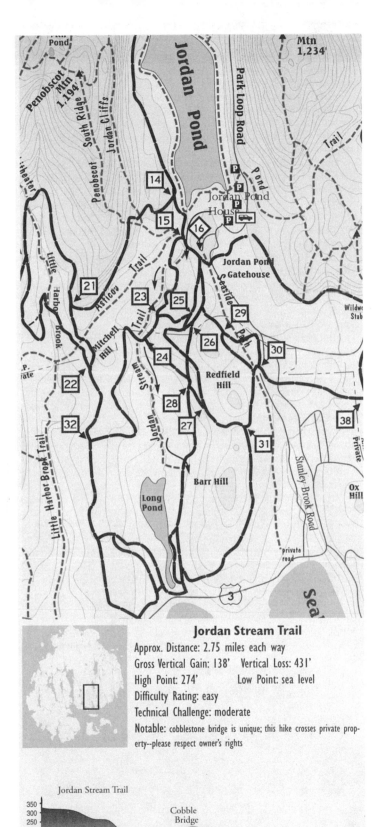

Jordan Stream Trail

Approx. Distance: 2.75 miles each way

Gross Vertical Gain: 138'   Vertical Loss: 431'

High Point: 274'   Low Point: sea level

Difficulty Rating: easy

Technical Challenge: moderate

Notable: cobblestone bridge is unique; this hike crosses private property--please respect owner's rights

I always wish I could do the Little Harbor Brook Trail more often. The best time to hike this trail is during peak foliage times (the same could be said of just about any trail), although any time of the year will do.

A number of mountain springs and streams converge on the side of Sargent Mountain to form Little Harbor Brook. This small stream flows 3.5 miles to the sea (at Little Harbor, no less) where its mouth forms something of an estuary, dominated by the tides.

Although open for public use, this trail lies partly on private land.

A small bridge spans Little Harbor Brook's estuary on route 3 near the sign marking the border between Seal Harbor and Northeast Harbor. The parking area for this hike lies just west of the bridge. A skinny signpost marks the 'Harbor Brook Trail' and the "Jordan Ridge" trail.[1] The trail cuts through a thick fir grove as it approaches the stream's edge. It stays along the stream for most of the next 1.7 miles.

This gently sloping trail has a narrow treadway, and thick woods line both sides. The Eliot Mtn East Face Trail (hike 3-31) branches left off the Harbor Brook Trail approximately one mile from Route 3. Shortly after this intersection the path meanders away from the brook's edge. It crosses a marsh-like stretch but rounds back to Harbor Brook. You will reach a long wooden bridge where the Harbor Brook Trail reaches the Asticou Trail.

Most other maps show the Little Harbor Brook trail's intersection with the Asticou trail incorrectly: The Little Harbor Brook Trail meets the bridge and the Asticou Trail on the left side of the stream. It does not cross the brook until it reaches the bridge. Take a right over the bridge and follow the Asticou Trail to the first carriage road and take a left. Follow this carriage road to the small granite bridge where you may resume hiking the trail along Little Harbor Brook. From this point on signs refer to the trail as Amphitheater Trail.

Now on park land, the rock-filled trail crosses the stream repeatedly during the next half mile. As it reaches another bridge (this one much larger and landscaped into the side of the earth), the trail rises to the carriage road (with the stream on the right), crosses the carriage road, and continues up Sargent Mountain.

After reaching the naturally formed Amphitheater area, cairns mark the trail as it veers steeply up and to the left. Past this point, the trail passes many super picnic areas whose southern and western exposures offer warm sun and great views of the Cranberry Isles and ocean. Higher up, you'll reach the intersection with the Sargent Mtn South Ridge Trail near Birch Spring and the Cedar Swamp Mountain trails (hike 3-25).

The top of Sargent lies about 1.2 miles up the trail to the right, as marked by signposts, cairns, and paint.

Sargent Mtn's broad dome lies at 1,373 f.a.s.l. The top portion of Sargent's South Ridge is among my favorite mountaintops.

The return trip down the same Amphitheater and Little Harbor Brook trails offers new and interesting perspectives of the water route along a fairly mild grade.

The start of the long & scenic Little Harbor Brook

---

1. Although abandoned today, phantoms have kept open the lower portions of this path connecting to Penobscot's south ridge.

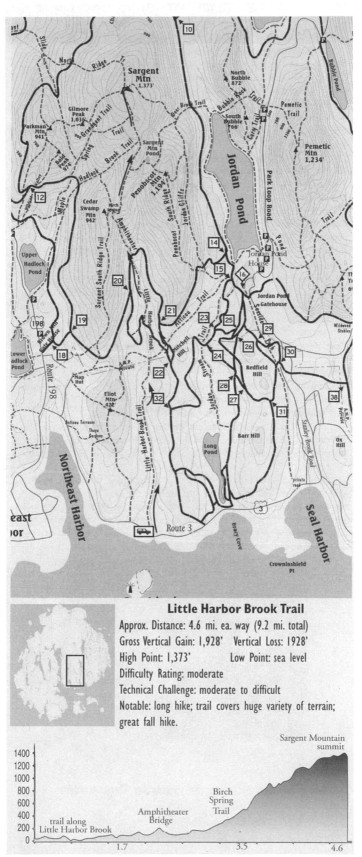

Little Harbor Brook Trail

Approx. Distance: 4.6 mi. ea. way (9.2 mi. total)

Gross Vertical Gain: 1,928'   Vertical Loss: 1928'

High Point: 1,373'   Low Point: sea level

Difficulty Rating: moderate

Technical Challenge: moderate to difficult

Notable: long hike; trail covers huge variety of terrain; great fall hike.

While some of the hikes found in this book traverse obscure trails, some hikes up Eliot Mtn seem downright arcane. Most maps fail to label the mountain. Of those that do label the peak, some still refer to it as "Savage Mt." Only a few maps show any trail to its peak, although at least four lead there.[1]

Eliot Mtn's trails are among the oldest recreational hiking paths on the island; some were built by the so-called Champlain Society, the group whose efforts began the drive to establish the national park and whose ideas still merit consideration.

This hike up Eliot forms a loop, returning to Rte 3 two-tenths of a mile up the road from the parking area. Eliot rises over Northeast Harbor and provides a haven for the Thuya Gardens, a wonderfully manicured garden. (This hike passes near this garden's walls, and a brief detour takes hikers into it.)

Park at the same area as the previous hike, at the mouth of Little Harbor Brook. The trail quickly narrows. It stays along the left side of the brook, meandering with it. The first sign post lies about three-quarters of a mile from the road. It marks the trail to Eliot Mtn, the gardens, and the Asticou Terraces, so follow this trail to the left.

It rises straight ahead, making slight curves, avoiding only the largest obstacles. A true woodland-style trail, small, moss-covered cairns mark the trail. It bends a bit more as it nears the top. As it swerves through low-bush blueberries and levels slightly the trail reaches another signpost.

The top of Eliot lies to the right of the sign, but there are no more 'significant' views beyond what you can see from this intersection: Northeast Harbor stretching into the ocean. When you continue this hike from this signpost, take a left. The trip down from this signpost drops quickly at first. To reach the gardens, take a right at the first sign you encounter, where the options are "up" or "Thuya Gardens and Asticou," followed by another right where the options are either "Rte 3" or "Thuya Gardens" and "Asticou."

The trail drops stair-style to yet another signpost which gives you the choice between "Gardens" or "parking." Choose the Gardens (to the right). Although the back door of the Gardens opens, a donation box is located at the front door.

Returning to the trail out the back door (by taking two left turns followed by a right and heading towards Rte 3 at the sign marking it), the wooded trail drops moderately. Soon, however, stones fill the trail and water often dampens the surface. Easy to follow but often wet, the trail drops to Rte 3 at the scrawny sign marking "Eliot Mtn" and "Trail." The original parking area lies two-tenths of a mile down Rte 3 to the left.

The front gates to the spectacular Thuya Gardens.

---

1. The mountain lies largely on private land, some of which is open to public use.

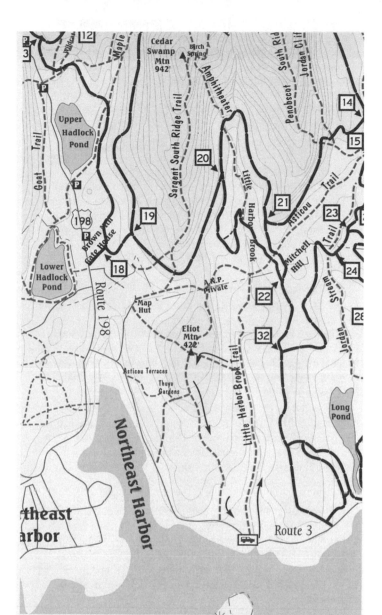

Eliot Mountain

Approx. Distance: 2.75 mi.

Gross Vertical Gain: 602' Vertical Loss: 602'

High Point: 422' Low Point: sea level

Difficulty Rating: moderate

Technical Challenge: moderate

Notable: Thuya Gardens. *please note:* private property rights apply!

89

An alternative hike up Eliot Mtn forms a loop starting from the Asticou area. It includes the Asticou Terraces as well as the Thuya Gardens.

Unique among all of Mount Desert Island's trails, the Asticou Terraces Trail was privately built and endowed. Private maintenance from that endowment continues today. A parking area for this trail lies a stone's throw from the Asticou Inn (on the Seal Harbor side of Route 3), 100 yards west of the inn.

The granite work involved in this trail is remarkable. Retaining and supporting walls of pink granite lie plainly visible from the road and parking area. Stairs of both natural stone and cut granite provide sure footing. Joseph Curtis, the landscape architect who designed, paid for, and endowed this path, spared no expense building it. Crews even blasted rock from the hillside to provide a better corridor for the trail.

Additionally, rustic huts were built of natural materials. These relics remain in place today, nestled into the hillside overlooking Northeast Harbor.

The path crosses an old road (today something of a maintenance path) as it continues to rise toward the Thuya Gardens. This maintenance path provides a connection to the Map Hut located at the end of the Asticou Trail near another woodland trail up Eliot Mountain's west shoulder (hike 3-23).

You will pass the Thuya Lodge before reaching the gardens. A relief map on the outside of the lodge provides some interesting details, but the real attraction lies behind the walls of the garden.

Inside, a beautifully landscaped garden has been maintained for decades. The small donation fee requested for entrance is well worth the price.

Hikers may choose to continue trekking through the woods near the gardens. There are two ways of accessing the same set of trails: either directly from the back of the gardens or by exiting the gardens, proceeding down the lodge's driveway (toward Route 3) and taking a left on the sign that says "trails." The second option leads to the trail reached from the back door of the garden discussed in the first option.

All of the trails in this neck of the woods are discussed in the previous hike description.

One of several cliff-side gazebos located on the Asticou Terraces Trail.

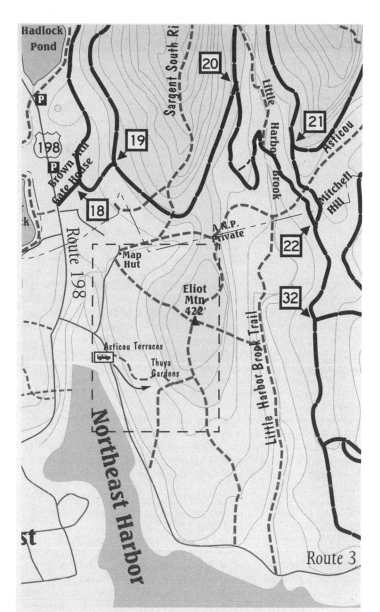

Asticou Terraces

Approx. Distance: .8 mi. or 2.2 mi.

Gross Vertical Gain: 465'   Vertical Loss: 465'

High Point: 400'   Low Point: sea level

Difficulty Rating: easy

Technical Challenge: easy

Notable: Thuya Gardens, gazebos on trails, Eliot Mtn.

Trails run around both Lower and Upper Hadlock Ponds. The noise of traffic on Route 198 can resonate in the valley east of Norumbega Mountain, but in the absence of such racket, hiking around these two ponds can be quite relaxing.

The trail running around Upper Hadlock Pond was built over 120 years ago by a group of Harvard students who called themselves The Champlain Society. After looking at this trail, you might wonder if it has received any upkeep since.

An old-style sign post that says TRAIL on the front and marks the trails around Upper Hadlock Pond and up Sargent Mtn leads into the woods from the gravel parking area located at the south end of Upper Hadlock. As it heads along the back side of Upper Hadlock Pond (especially closer to the south end) erosion has taken its toll, leaving roots highly exposed.

Toward the northern end of Upper Hadlock Pond the trail's surface becomes much nicer. It bends away from the pond, crossing two small streams near the trail leading to Hadlock Brook Trail and Maple Spring Trail (hike 3-37).

Take a left at the first sign post. This short trail leads to Route 198. It crosses Route 198 to the Norumbega trailhead. A cedar post marks this trail on the other side of the parking area. Take another left turn just inside the woods. This left turn extends the Goat Trail[1] toward Lower Hadlock Pond.

It runs along the eastern base of Norumbega and possesses aspects that are unique within the island's trail system. Blue paint marks the trail. Moss covers much of the forest and virtually all rock surfaces.

A signpost marks a trail that leads back to the parking area. This trail bears to the left. I recommend staying to the right. This trail to the right extends toward Lower Hadlock Pond.

Lower Hadlock lies a short distance to the right from the next intersection. Nice waterfalls and a picturesque arched foot bridge mark this trail's meeting with Lower Hadlock. The parking area lies to the left of the Goat Trail's intersection, so if you desire to return to the original parking area for this hike, take a left. The trail follows the side of the brook that connects Upper and Lower Hadlock Ponds.

It is possible to circle Lower Hadlock Pond in either direction from the footbridge, however. The Northeast Harbor Village Improvement Society continues to improve and maintain this pleasant shoreline trail.

At the southwest end of the pond, the trail passes the Shady Hill Trail (hike 3-39) which runs up the south ridge of Norumbega Mountain. Additionally, trails extend from the other side of the brick building at the dam. These trails extend into the privately maintained Northeast Harbor system.

It is easy to make a complete loop around Lower Hadlock, although my experience has been that it takes longer than you might think to circle this small pond.

Most other maps show this area incorrectly!

Bald Peak and Sargent Mountain rise over Upper Hadlock Pond

---

1. This trail was formerly known as the Notch Trail.; a sign still directs hikers to "Notch Trail" along the lower portion of the Hadlock Brook Trail (see next hike).

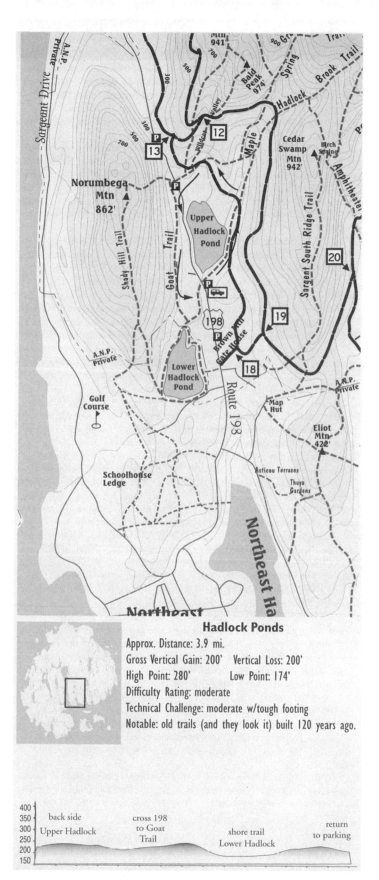

Hadlock Ponds

Approx. Distance: 3.9 mi.

Gross Vertical Gain: 200'   Vertical Loss: 200'

High Point: 280'   Low Point: 174'

Difficulty Rating: moderate

Technical Challenge: moderate w/tough footing

Notable: old trails (and they look it) built 120 years ago.

This challenging hike forms a loop on the west side of Sargent Mountain. I really enjoy the trails described in this hike. I often play a game with myself speculating where I would put a house or cabin were I offered anyplace in the park, including a coastal location, a mountaintop spot, or a wooded hide-away. There is a spot on the Maple Spring Trail I would seriously consider for the latter.

This hike begins and ends on the Hadlock Brook Trail, starting just north of Upper Hadlock Pond. Park on the west side of 1998 (the Norumbega Mountain parking area) but begin this hike on the east side (Upper Hadlock's side).

Past the large cedar post, the trail passes over a rocky area that looks like a river bed. You will pass the Parkman Mtn trail on the left, the Bald Peak Trail on the left, and cross a carriage road in the first quarter mile, staying on the Hadlock Brook Trail.

Continuing across the carriage road, the trail rises into the woods, running along shelf between two extremely steep behemoth stone surfaces. At the intersection where three small signs nailed into the sides of large trees have messages of "Notch Trail," "Upper Hadlock Trail" (to the right), and "to Sargent Mtn" to the left; take this left.

The trail drops slowly over fair surfaces and reaches a signpost that marks the split between Maple Spring and Hadlock Brook Trails. Take a left onto Maple Spring Trail. It rises then falls toward a gurgling mountain brook. Rugged footing becomes the norm. The trail drops to the brook's edge and crosses it, rising away from the opposite bank via granite steps. It stays along the right side of the brook as it cuts a deeper swath into the earth. It then crosses below the Maple Spring carriage road bridge.

I'd put my imaginary cottage just past the bridge on the right side of the stream. Scenic, high crags of rocks form the edges of the brook as it zig-zags up a steep valley. Flat-topped stones provide a fairly reliable surface for walking as the trail crosses back to the left side of the brook.

·The trail passes the end of the Giant Slide Trail (hike 3-43) where a sign marks Bald Peak & Parkman Mtn to the left (hike 3-39). Maple Spring Trail continues straight. It crosses back to the right side and rises steeply as the stones along the trail become round and loose among themselves. When the trail veers away from the brook, glance to the northwest and see if you can see the steep southeast side of Gilmore Peak towering above the trail.

Maple Spring Trail rises over a knoll then, when Sargent's South Ridge appears, the trail drops into the valley between these two ridges. A small sign marks Maple Spring. The trail rises steeply from this point to the broad south ridge of Sargent Mtn. Bald Peak and Parkman appear to the southwest.

The trail continues up along smooth rock. The top of Sargent appears from the intersection with the Sargent Mtn Trail.

To descend along the Hadlock Brook Trail return down the Sargent South Ridge Trail. Pass the Maple Spring signpost and take a right at the next one ("Birch Spring" and "Rte 198 parking"). The trail drops steeply, mostly over smooth rock as it runs off the south ridge of the mountain and into fairly thick woods. The steep drop can be challenging. The trail reaches an intersection with the Cedar Swamp Mountain trail (hike 3-29).

Continue straight ahead over loose rocks, bare and exposed root systems, and the bed of Hadlock Brook itself.

The trail crosses over a carriage road on the right side of the bridge. This bridge has several turrets and stands as another impressive architectural structure. (The Maple Spring bridge appears to the right along the carriage road.)

The trail drops down to the right and cuts away from the brook. Two stepping stone bridges precede a signpost already encountered on this hike. Take a left and repeat the first section of the hike, dropping back to Rte198.

1.Hadlock Brook Trail, formerly known as the Waterfall Trail, was a logging road for at least 50 years before the Northeast Harbor VIS extended it and turned it into a hiking trail near the turn of the century.

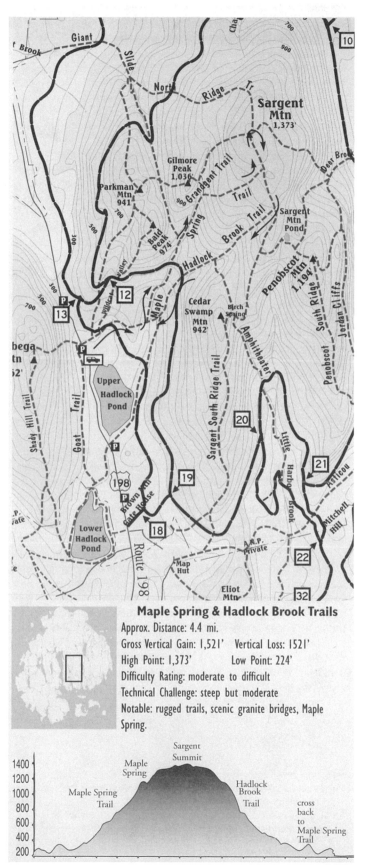

Maple Spring & Hadlock Brook Trails

Approx. Distance: 4.4 mi.

Gross Vertical Gain: 1,521'   Vertical Loss: 1521'

High Point: 1,373'   Low Point: 224'

Difficulty Rating: moderate to difficult

Technical Challenge: steep but moderate

Notable: rugged trails, scenic granite bridges, Maple Spring.

Parkman Mtn and Bald Peak jut out of the western shoulder of Sargent Mountain. While many trails lead to the tops of these two peaks, the loop described here gives hikers the most varied terrain and avoids unnecessarily steep descents. This route starts along the Hadlock Brook, Maple Spring, and Giant Slide Trails using the same parking area and following the same first 3/4 mile that begins the Maple Spring and Hadlock Brook Hike (3-37).[1]

Proceed straight ahead along the Maple Spring and Hadlock Brook Trails. Along the way you pass three signs on the left marking trails up either Parkman, Bald, or both, but continue along the Maple Spring Trail. After crossing a carriage road and rising to a trail split where three wooden signs are nailed into three large trees, follow the trail to the left (toward "Sargent Mtn"). This is the Maple Spring Trail.

It drops and reaches yet another split, but continue straight ahead. Layers of pine needles collected on the forest floor have softened the trail as it swerves around rocks and trees. It drops to the side of a brook, crosses it, and rises along the right side of the brook. The Maple Spring Trail reaches the huge bridge that is part of the "Around the Mountain" carriage loop. The Maple Spring Trail crosses below the bridge. The trail crosses the stream to avoid some of the jagged (ouch!) rocks that form the trail's surface along the brook.

Just past the bridge another sign marks Bald Peak and Parkman Mtn. (Although no mention is made, this trail to the left is the western terminus of the Giant Slide trail). Follow it to the left. Extremely rocky, the trail runs between Bald Peak and Parkman Mtn on one side, and Gilmore Peak and Sargent Mtn on the other.[2] At the next signpost follow the trail to the left up to the top of Parkman Mtn.

The trail rises straight up the back side of Parkman. This rapid rise reveals great vistas in all directions, including Gilmore Peak and Sargent Mtn to the northeast, Norumbega and Somes Sound to the west, and Bald Peak to the southeast. Additional views include a straight shot to Northeast Harbor down Route 198 to the south, as well as the flat lands near Upper Hadlock Pond, parts of Somes Sound to the west and north, and the scantily clad mountains in the area.

Several trails run back to the parking area. A short trail connects the tops of Parkman and Bald. If you choose to go to the top of Bald Peak, a steep trail drops off the southwest side of that peak and runs back to the first trail section of this hike. Another trail runs back to the starting area across Parkman's southwest face. Similar in nature to the southwest face of Bald Peak, but much less steep. This trail starts down from the signpost that lies between Parkman Mtn and Bald Peak. It drops gradually back to the parking area, swerving across the side of Parkman.

---

1. The park service has a "Parkman Mtn parking area" on Route 198, but no trail up the mountain starts from it.

2. This valley was among the last to be without trails. The 1928 path guide of Mount Desert Island recommended this area for those interested in exploring wild valleys without the aid of a trail *per se*.

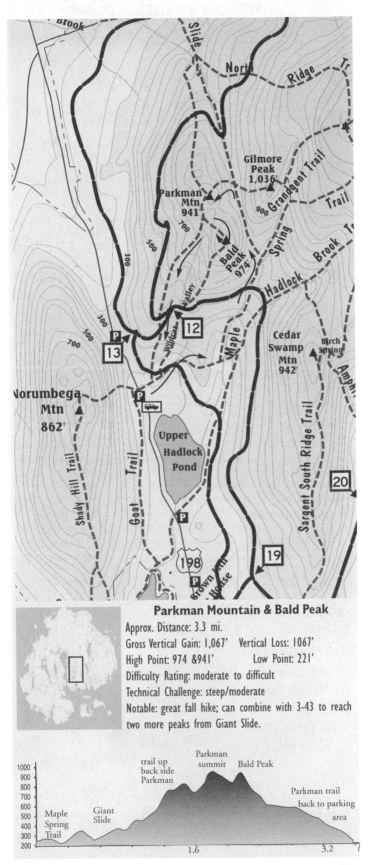

Parkman Mountain & Bald Peak

Approx. Distance: 3.3 mi.

Gross Vertical Gain: 1,067'   Vertical Loss: 1067'

High Point: 974 &941'   Low Point: 221'

Difficulty Rating: moderate to difficult

Technical Challenge: steep/moderate

Notable: great fall hike; can combine with 3-43 to reach two more peaks from Giant Slide.

Norumbega rises along the east side of Somes Sound directly across the sound from Flying Mtn, Valley Peak, St. Sauveur Mtn and Acadia Mtn. Norumbega reaches the greatest height of the four, and its relatively long ridge parallels the sound for nearly a mile.

Like its counterparts across the sound, Norumbega's proximity to the water allows it to offer broad, unobstructed vistas of local coastlines and beyond. The trail starts from the back of the parking lot and rises rapidly through thick woods with alarming alacrity; in less than a quarter mile it gains about 600 vertical feet. I believe this section of trail is one of the most challenging in the whole system. The trail makes a sweeping left turn toward the summit; the rock to rock surface demands effort and attention.

Vistas expand greatly as the trail clears the steep area and the tree line. The flat section bordering the northern area of Hadlock Pond appears below, and to the west, the stark tops of Parkman Mtn, Bald Peak, and Gilmore Peak dominate the rocky area along Sargent's west side. The trail makes cutbacks along the flat top of the mountain as it rises to the peak, marked only by a huge pile of stones.[1]

The sound's waters run deep and dark to both the north and south. Miles of views appear in all directions. A unique panorama of the island's south end appears distorted by the rapid slope of Eliot Mtn's slant into the ocean along Northeast Harbor's coast. The steep, rocky sides of the small mountains across the sound contrast with the rest of the southwest coast which appears flat as it stretches south past the Seawall area to the Bass Harbor Lighthouse.

The trail continues southward along the ridge, parallel to the sound. Follow the trail to the left at the intersection. The spur to the right drops to the Northeast Harbor Golf Course.

The Shady Hill Trail's surface changes from rocky to needle covered. The gradual descent offers great hiking as it drops slowly to Lower Hadlock Pond (see hike 3-35).

Follow the trail to the left along the back side of Lower Hadlock Pond. At the waterfall bear to the left along the brook. Take another left on the Goat Trail[2] about 150 yards from the waterfall. This trail runs along the lower east edge of Norumbega for almost a mile. Tightly enclosed by thick woods, the footing remains good, but the trail can be difficult to follow. There is one sharp right turn to a parking area at the southern end of Hadlock Pond. Skip this turn.

Route 198 parallels the trail. The rumble of vehicles along 198 reminds hikers of the road, but the powerful smell of firs dominates between the roar of trucks. At the final trail intersection turn right to the parking area.

The Brown Mountain Gate House, gateway to the area carriage road, lies just south of the parking area of this hike.

---

1. Don't be fooled by other large cairns you may spy along the upper ridge of Norumbega; some mark trails that are now abandoned.

2. Although a sign directs you to the Goat Trail, this carry trail along the lower eastern edge of Norumbega is the old Notch Trail; Upper Hadlock Pond was formerly known as Lake Notch.

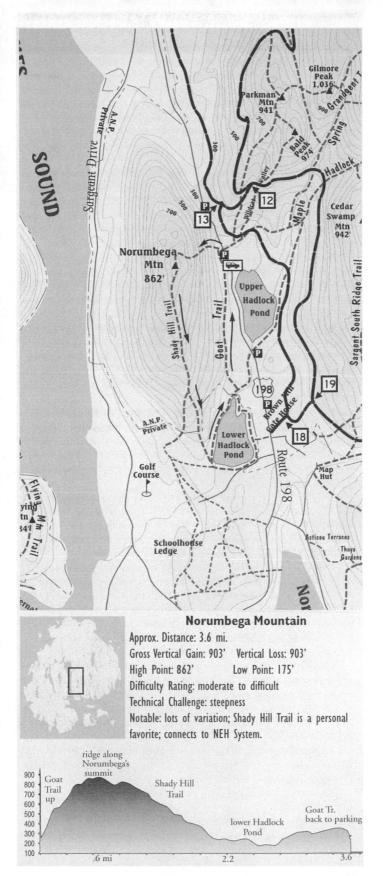

Norumbega Mountain

Approx. Distance: 3.6 mi.

Gross Vertical Gain: 903'   Vertical Loss: 903'

High Point: 862'   Low Point: 175'

Difficulty Rating: moderate to difficult

Technical Challenge: steepness

Notable: lots of variation; Shady Hill Trail is a personal favorite; connects to NEH System.

Heading north on Route 198 from Northeast Harbor, a cedar post marks the Giant Slide Trail on the right side of the road, just north of Sargeant Drive. Hikers must park along Route 198 and walk the three tenths of a mile to the trailhead. The Giant Slide Trail follows an intense route to the top of the island's second highest peak over varied terrains; this is the only hike in this book that passes over Gilmore Peak. Giant Slide Trail slices through Sargent Brook's gaping boulders, and the hiking is often highly challenging.

A cedar post marks the start of the actual trail at the top of the road to Route 198. After another 3/10ths mile, it crosses the seldom used carriage road that connects the Hadlock Pond area to the Aunt Betty's Pond area. On the other side of the carriage road the trail's direction changes from east to south, and the footing becomes more difficult; rocks and roots clutter the trail as it parallels the Sargent Brook.

The Giant Slide Trail runs along the edge brook, crossing over and under monolithic boulders. The trail passes a signpost (Sargent Mtn's North Ridge on the left; Parkman Mtn, Bald Peak and Maple Spring to the right), but you should continue straight. No other trail offers such singularly dynamic hiking.

Blue paint splotches mark the trail along with occasional metal blue diamonds at eye level in the trees. Giant Slide levels before it crosses the "Around the Mountain" carriage loop and drops into the woods again. Fairly level and often moist, the trail reaches a signpost. This sign marks the only trail up Gilmore Peak, a trail called The Grandgent Trail.[1] Follow this trail to the left.

The steep climb to Gilmore Peak offers views of Parkman and Bald Mtn, as well as Sargent Mtn, Somes Sound, and Northeast Harbor. The journey to the top of Sargent continues by backtracking slightly from the top of Gilmore Peak and dropping into the valley between Gilmore and Sargent. The narrow trail reaches a brook. Take a left along the narrow trail.

After a short flat section, the trail becomes unabashedly steep. It rises up Sargent along the rocky riverbed. Its course between the Sargent Mountain North Ridge Trail and the Maple Spring Trail (to which it originally connected at a lower level) is the most challenging trail up Sargent. After clearing the tree line the trail rises to Sargent's peak.

The views from the top of Sargent are tremendous. Both of the recently mentioned trails, the North Ridge and the Maple Spring, return to the Giant Slide. I recommend going down the North Ridge Trail. The North Ridge Trail drops mostly over smooth rock until it reaches the "Around the Mountain" carriage loop, crosses it, and drops steeply back to Giant Slide. The North Ridge Trail offers excellent views of Somes Sound and the northern sections of MDI.

Alternatively, you may choose to descend via Sargent's South Ridge Trail to the Maple Spring Trail. The Maple Spring trail begins at the first right turn (well marked by a signpost) off the South Ridge Trail. It drops steeply, rock to rock, along a brook. The first signpost directs hikers to Parkman Mtn and Bald Peak. This intersection also marks extreme end of the Giant Slide.

Following this trail to the right will bring you past the Parkman cutoff on the left and the Grandgent Trail on the right. From here, the first mile of the hike repeats itself in reverse.

---

1. Named after former Southwest Harbor VIA path committee chairman, Charles Grandgent who built the trail; see the book *Trails of History* for the whole story.

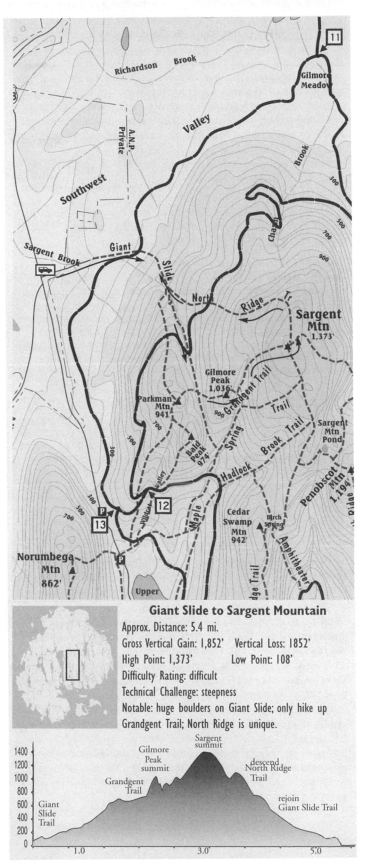

Richardson Brook

Gilmore Meadow

Valley

Chasm Brook

Southwest

A.N.P. Private

Sargent Brook

Giant Slide

North Ridge Tr

Sargent Mtn 1,373'

Gilmore Peak 1,036

Parkman Mtn 941

Grandgent Trail

Sargent Mtn Pond

Penobscot Mtn 1,194

Bald Peak 974

Spring

Hadlock Brook Trail

Valley

Maple

Cedar Swamp Mtn 942'

Birch Spring

Amphitheater

Norumbega Mtn 862'

Ridge Trail

Upper

Giant Slide to Sargent Mountain

Approx. Distance: 5.4 mi.

Gross Vertical Gain: 1,852'   Vertical Loss: 1852'

High Point: 1,373'   Low Point: 108'

Difficulty Rating: difficult

Technical Challenge: steepness

Notable: huge boulders on Giant Slide; only hike up Grandgent Trail; North Ridge is unique.

Sargent summit

Gilmore Peak summit

descend North Ridge Trail

Grandgent Trail

Giant Slide Trail

rejoin Giant Slide Trail

1400
1200
1000
800
600
400
200
0

1.0   3.0   5.0

IV. Region Four–Western Mountain

The Western Mountain hikers are characterized by serene, uncrowded woods. Most of the mountains on this side of the island have tree covered peaks; vistas from overlooks are more readily available. The region offers quiet, uncrowded hiking. The trails in this area were originally established as hiking trails *per se* by the Southwest Harbor Village Improvement Association, although individuals from each of the other village improvement associations and societies have taken credit for the building of some west side trails.

In fact, the lion's share of trail building in this region was performed by the CCC during the 1930s. Works of this agency continue to benefit all hikers of the Western Mountains.

Included in this region are both my favorite loop in the park, titled *Western Mountain Hike*, and one of the finest trails the island has ever seen, The Perpendicular Trail.

Hike	Name	Parking	Level
4-1	Great Pond Trail	Long Pond	moderate
4-3	Perpendicular	Long Pond	difficult
4-5	Western Mtn Hike	Long Pond	difficult
4-7	Sluiceway/SouthFace	Mill Field	difficult
4-9	Bernard West Ledge	Western Mtn.Rd	moderate
4-11	Beech Cliffs Ladder	Echo Lake Beach	difficult
4-13	Beech Mountain	Beech Hill Road	moderate
4-15	Canada Cliffs	Beech Hill Road	moderate
4-17	Valley Trail	Long Pond	moderate

Directions to Parking

Long Pond parking: on 102, south of Echo Lake, and just past the food mart, take a right onto Seal Cove Road, followed by a right on Long Pond Road; follow to end, park at pumping station.

Mill Field: follow directions above to Seal Cove Road, but instead of taking a right on Long Pond Road, follow Seal Cove Road straight ahead; take a right after the campground, followed by another right, then follow signs to Mill Field (a left turn).

Western Mountain Road: from 102- right on Seal Cove Road, follow for several miles, pass Long Pond Road and signs to Mill Field. Right, then left on Western Mountain Road to trailhead.

Echo Lake Beach: off route 102 on the island's west side, a park service sign marks the parking area. (Restrooms near beach, phone in parking lot)

Beech Hill Road parking: heading south through Somesville on route 102, follow signs to Beech Mountain by taking a right at the white fire house. Take a left onto Beech Hill Road (following park service sign indicating Beech Mtn.)

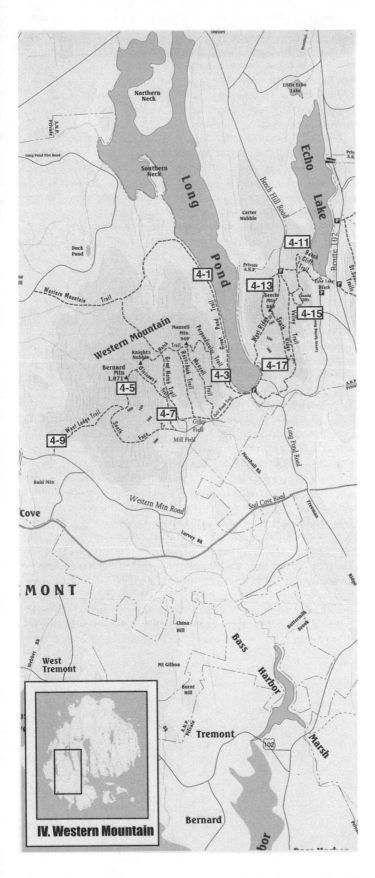

The trail along the west shore of Long Pond stands as the finest trail along a freshwater body on the entire island. It runs for two miles along the western shore, skirting along the front side of Mansell Mtn until leaving the side of Long Pond (known for many years as 'Great Pond').

Among the most "rustic" trails found on the island, The Great Pond Trail starts at the pump station and passes The Cold Brook Trail (where a cedar post marks one way up Mansell Mtn), continues over a brief rocky area, and passes the start of The Perpendicular Trail (hike 4-3). Beyond Perpendicular it offers great, fairly easy hiking for more than one and one-half miles along the pond.[1]

A supporting wall of natural, uncut stone runs along the entire length of the path, while split granite culverts provide proper drainage for the trail. Most erosion problems have eluded this well-built trail. Also, the trail stays wide enough for two most of the way. Wooden and stone bridges span small streams running off Mansell's east side. Smooth, soft footing continues along most of the trail.

After two miles along Long Pond, the trail cuts west into the woods. Good footing continues along the first section after the turn. Beyond the wooded foot bridge, however, hiking becomes more challenging. ANP trail crews have repaired most of the trail surfaces as it rises along Great Brook. The trail meets a signpost about 1/2 mile from Long Pond. From the sign post take a right to continue this hike, heading toward the Long Pond Fire Road. This trail is properly known as the Pine Hill Trail. Pine Hill lies at the end of this trail.

While erosion makes the hiking difficult in places (especially when the trail gets wet), the trail has a strong positive point: it cuts through some of the nicest woods found on the island. Firs dominate, and their green and brown colorings lend a unique atmosphere to the trail. The trail levels as it leaves the thick grove and cuts through low bush blueberries. It runs across sections of smooth rock, but in between this ancient trail has cut deeply into the earth (8-12 inches is deep for a trail). Again, this depression can fill with water.

It reaches the 'Long Pond Fire Road' (also known as Hodgon Pond Road) at a cedar post. This road extends up to Long Pond's northwestern shore, the Pretty Marsh area to the right, and out between Hodgon Pond and Seal Cove Pond to the left. Virtually all of this road is part of Acadia National Park. No other trail connection can be made from here, so you must return by the same way you came, but that's not all bad.

---

1. See the book *Trails of History* for the story of who built this trail and why.

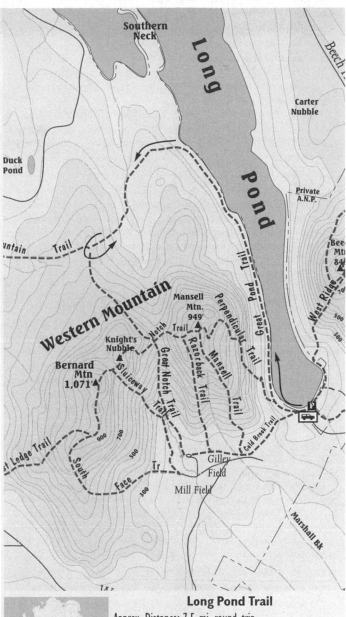

Long Pond Trail

Approx. Distance: 7.5 mi. round trip

Gross Vertical Gain: 792'   Vertical Loss: 792'

High Point: 400'   Low Point: 70'

Difficulty Rating: easy to moderate

Technical Challenge: easy

Notable: the best lake-shore trail on the island; Pine Hill Trail is as quiet as can be.

The Perpendicular Trail stands as a masterpiece in trail building. Although first shown on maps as early as 1918, the trail as it appears today was built by the CCC.[1]

The Western Mountain area of Acadia receives far less use than the east side of the island. Mansell and Bernard make up the bulk of the tract and are the two highest peaks there. The stair step craftsmanship of the Perpendicular Trail up Mansell Mtn makes it a special place on the island.

From the pumping station at the south end of Long Pond follow the Great Pond Trail around the pond to the left. Perpendicular starts two-tenths of a mile from the pump house. Stairs start almost immediately, and hundreds of solid granite steps follow the first one.

Granite coping lines both sides of this solidly built trail, forming some of the most picturesque stretches in the park. The pseudo-spiral staircase and the associated reshaping of Mansell's face may be the single most remarkable feat of trail construction ever accomplished on Mount Desert Island.

One small ladder and three iron rungs lie midway up the mountain. After a flat section that includes a long, large supporting wall, the trail changes.

It assumes a woodland style, skirts along the bases of huge boulders, crosses a small stream and passes the trail's best overlook. The trail then cuts inland to the top of Mansell. Marked simply by a sign post, there are no vistas from the top. The trail continues through dark woods to an intersection.

Follow the trail to the right, marked by signs to Knights Nubble and The Great Notch. (The Mansell Trail which extends straight ahead from this intersection drops steeply its entire length, reaching Gilley Field and the last stretch of the new Cold Brook Trail). The trail to the right also drops steeply in spurts. After skirting up a short steep rock knoll, it reaches another sign post. Follow the Razorback Trail to the left. It descends across smooth rock folds and offers great views of the broad valley in Western Mountain.

Lower, Razorback enters pine filled woods and continues its steep descent. Small cairns and metal birds in trees mark the trail. (Unlike many of the island's mountains, neither Mansell nor Bernard have trails that descend gradually along their south ridges.) Razorback ends at its intersection with the Cold Brook Trail near Gilley Field.

Another CCC project, the Cold Brook Trail provides a causeway that links many of the trails in Western Mountain.[2] It extends from the bottom of the Bernard Mtn South Face Trail to the pumping house at Long Pond (although it is interrupted once by the Western Mountain Road near Gilley Field). Follow the Cold Brook Trail to the left. It drops quickly back to Long Pond, running across rocks and roots as it drops back to the pump house.

One of my favorite stretches along the upper section of the Perpendicular Trail

1. The CCC established a camp at Great Pond and performed extensive trail work in the Western Mountain tract. More than thirty pages of the book *Trails of History* are dedicated to the work of the CCC, including 34 previously unpublished photos of the work and workmen of this New Deal program that rebuilt much of Acadia.

2. Much of the original Cold Brook Trail now lies abandoned; the wide 'substitute' Cold Brook Trail provides much of the same passage as the original path.

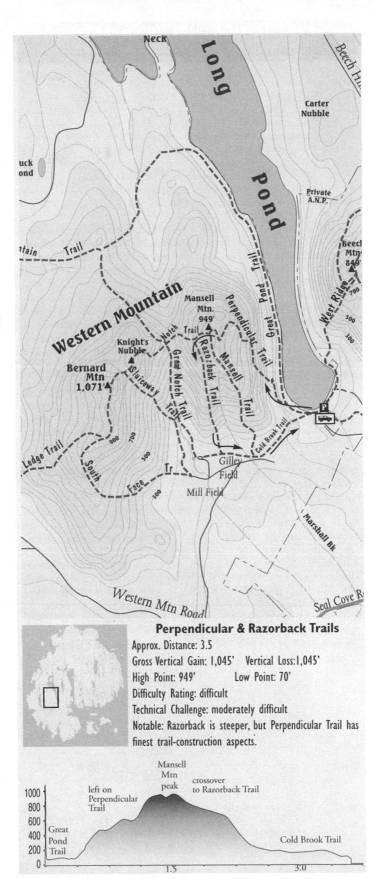

Perpendicular & Razorback Trails

Approx. Distance: 3.5

Gross Vertical Gain: 1,045' Vertical Loss: 1,045'

High Point: 949' Low Point: 70'

Difficulty Rating: difficult

Technical Challenge: moderately difficult

Notable: Razorback is steeper, but Perpendicular Trail has finest trail-construction aspects.

Cedar posts mark trails in both directions from the pump house at Long Pond. The trails to the right lead to Beech Mountain and the Echo Lake area. To the left, trails head toward the Western Mountain area, a large, seldom-used section of Acadia.

Designed, planned, laid out, and constructed by professional and park service landscape architects, (including George Dorr himself, at the ripe old age of 84) the network of trails all connect easily to the starting point at the pump house. [1]

Go to the left behind the pump house. (The first of three trails climbing the slope of the Western Mountains, the Cold Brook Trail, starts from the parking lot. The second, known as the Perpendicular Trail, jets up to the left after another two-tenths of a mile.)

Well groomed and wide enough for two, the trail bends away from the side of the pond and rises into the woods after over two miles of shore-side hiking. The footing deteriorates after the small foot bridge over Great Pond Brook. Erosion has bared many rocks along a steep, often damp section.[2]

The trail meets the trail to the Long Pond Fire Road which veers to the right, but the hike continues on to the left. The woods around the path change dramatically after this turn. A forest of older pines grows along the next section. While they look and smell nice, their exposed root systems reek havoc on the trail. The trail rises and falls repeatedly for the next mile. A wooden box nailed into a tree and a sign post mark the intersection of several trails: Mansell Mtn to the left, Gilley Field straight ahead, and Knights Nubble & Bernard Mtn to the right. Take this right.

The next stretch challenges hikers. It cuts across and then straight up a steep, rocky face. After passing an overlook and the peak of Knights Nubble, the trail falls (to an intersection with the Sluiceway Trail), then rises steeply again past another overlook. The next overlook (on the right side of the trail) provides the nicest views of the hike: Indian Point, Bartlett's and other islands, along with the many coves and harbors of Mount Desert Island's west shore. An overlook on the left offers views of the ocean and the island's southwest lobe.

The hike continues over the nondescript top of Bernard, dropping over smooth rock and then into a patch of most excellent woods. The trail down is known as the Bernard South Face Trail. It weaves between the trees, swerving randomly through various types of woods. Stay left at the cedar post marking the West Ledge Trail (see hike 4-9).

After a prolonged steep drop, it crosses a single bridge and reaches the Bernard Mtn parking area at Mill Field where cedar posts mark both the South Face Trail and the Sluiceway Trail up Bernard (hike 4-7). This hike continues along the dirt road. Take a left onto the Western Mtn Road, followed by another left toward the 'reservoir' from where you can pick up the (unmarked) Cold Brook Trail. The Cold Brook Trail connects the trails in the area and passes the Mansell Mtn Trail, the Razorback Trail, and drops back to the shore of Long Pond at the pumping station approximately one mile from the tiny reservoir.

---

1. The CCC camp, NP-2, or the Great Pond Camp, was located near the pump house. It served as a natural hub to the trail system built in this area by the "C's."

2. This small, isolated rectangular section is still privately owned. The poor condition of this trail may be related to the CCC being restricted from working on private land; during the 'Acadia Expansion Program' in the 1930s, Dorr tried to acquire as much of the Western Mtn tract as possible; not all of it was for sale, however. See *Trails of History* for the whole story.

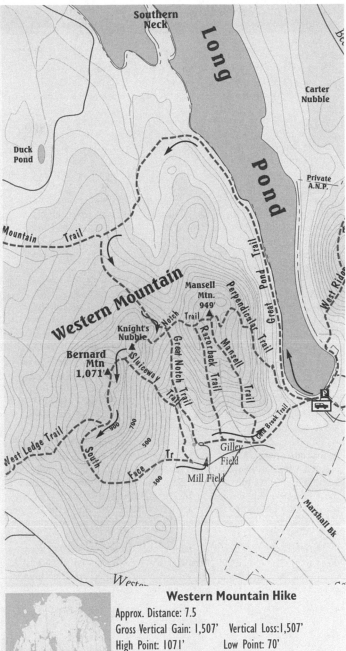

Southern
Neck

Long Pond

Carter
Nubble

Private
A.N.P.

Duck
Pond

Mountain   Trail

West Ridge

Western Mountain

Mansell Mtn.
949'

Perpendicular Trail

Great Pond Trail

Knight's
Nubble

Notch   Trail

Great Notch Trail

Razorback Trail

Mansell Trail

Bernard
Mtn
1,071'

Sluiceway Trail

West Ledge Trail

900 700 500
300

South   Face   Tr

Gilley
Field

Cold Brook Trail

Mill Field

Marshall Bk

Western

Western Mountain Hike

Approx. Distance: 7.5

Gross Vertical Gain: 1,507'   Vertical Loss: 1,507'

High Point: 1071'   Low Point: 70'

Difficulty Rating: moderate

Technical Challenge: moderately difficult

Notable: my favorite loop, but has no mountain-top views, *per se*. Great loop.

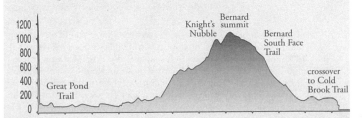

Great Pond Trail

Knight's
Nubble

Bernard
summit

Bernard
South Face
Trail

crossover
to Cold
Brook Trail

1200 1000 800 600 400 200 0

SLUICEWAY & SOUTH FACE TRAILS
challenging wooded trails in quiet area

Another of the ultra-quiet Western Mountain hikes, the Sluiceway Trail is one I usually hike rather than run. I enjoy it most for the terrain it covers over its upper sections. Filled with coniferous trees, these areas look almost the same year round. Cedar posts mark both the Sluiceway and South Face Trails from the parking area. I recommend following the Sluiceway Trail on the right.

From the parking area the trail rises gradually at first but soon assumes an almost constant steepness. The footing in these pine-dominated woods could be described as dubious as best.[1] For the most part the trail follows a packed surface of needles that covers the small rocks and roots in the area. The stream gurgles in the woods to the left, while higher up another stream converges on the trail along with the Mansell Mtn Trail.

A crossover to the Mansell Mtn Trail marks Sluiceway's crossing of the small brook. Following the Mansell Trail takes you to the Great Notch (between Knight's Nubble and Mansell Mtn) while continuing along Sluiceway (by bearing to the left) takes hikers between Knight's Nubble and Bernard Mtn at Little Notch (hike 4-3, Perpendicular & Razorback, runs over the ridge to the east from this intersection).

From Little Notch the hike continues to the left, rising to the "peak" of Bernard Mtn. Overlooks on either side of the trail provide the best vistas from the west side's highest peak. Past the overlooks the hike crosses short sections of smooth rock at the top of Bernard and drops into the woods along the South Face Trail.[2]

The footing on the way down changes often along with the general surroundings. The trail rounds the west side of the mountain and offers a couple glimpses of the flat area extending across Tremont and into Blue Hill Bay to the west. The woods near the top of Bernard make the South Face Trail part of my favorite hike on this side of the island. Thick as can be, sections of woods near the top remain dark even on the brightest summer days, offering an atmosphere difficult to find elsewhere on the island.

Stay to the left at the cedar post marking the Bernard West Ledge Trail. Further down the trail drops steadily through various types of woods, including an old apple orchard. (It passes two more abandoned trails as it descends. Both trails once led to the shore of Seal Cove Pond and were built as part of the Acadia Expansion Program by the CCC; old-style posts - minus their signs - remain on the side of the South Face Trail. Other trails built by the CCC provided connections to nearby Western Mountain trails, but are now phantom paths.)

As Bernard South Face winds back to the parking area at Mill Field it drops steeply to a small footbridge that spans the brook that parallels Sluiceway on the way up. After passing extensive water-bar construction the trail smooths and levels as it reaches the parking area.

---

1. An "abandoned" series of stone stairs provides possibly the best footing along the upper portion of this trail; you may inadvertently find yourself along these stairs without even trying. The story behind the abandonment of these stairs is dubious as well.

2. Although non-descript, it is interesting to note the old iron found on top of Bernard. These are remnants of a summer cottage that once graced the top of Bernard (in the not too distant past). A trail circled the top of the mountain (which the abandoned stone steps discussed in the previous footnote were a part of) and was named Kaighn Trail, in honor of the man whose cottage lay on the mountain top but who still welcomed hikers to use a trail that literally went across his doorstep.

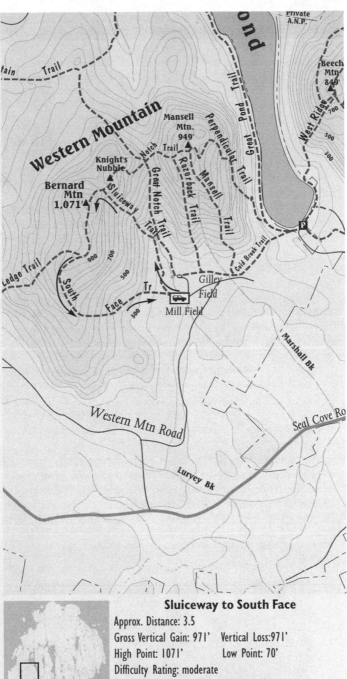

Sluiceway to South Face

Approx. Distance: 3.5

Gross Vertical Gain: 971'   Vertical Loss: 971'

High Point: 1071'   Low Point: 70'

Difficulty Rating: moderate

Technical Challenge: moderately difficult

Notable: nice, dark hike in the woods; remote area of Acadia; Sluiceway Trail is great year-round.

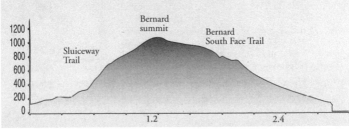

In the early 1990's, there seemed to be a problem with so-called 'trail phantoms.' Allegedly, these "phantoms" engaged in vigilante trail work, opening abandoned trails and building new ones where they felt needs existed.

Officials frowned upon this type of Mr.Fixit activity by private citizens in a national park. Most citizens opposed the work of the phantoms, and I did as well.

This did not deter some individuals from continuing to work, however. One person actually got caught.

The West Ledge Trail of Bernard is without question, an exception to the rule regarding phantom trail work. The work on this trail apparently served a need, so when the trail restoration work was discovered, officials decided to re-incorporate the trail into the system rather than re-obliterate the path. If an unwitting hiker followed this trail after encountering it on another hike, the hiker would be in for a long walk along Western Mountain Road to reach any other trailhead.

The West Ledge Trail starts on Western Mountain Road near the east side of Seal Cove Pond. With the possible exception of the Pine Hill Trail that skirts up Western Mountain a couple miles further north, the West Ledge Trail may be the most remote trail in the system.

Great views of Seal Cove Pond appear at low elevations. Further west, West Tremont extends in front of Blue Hill Bay.

The trail tends to rise steeply in short spurts, followed by relatively level sections that skirt humps in the back side of Bernard. As the trail approaches the tree line, it rises straight up the mountain's contour.

The trail intersects with Bernard's South Face Trail (see hikes 4-5 and 4-7). Take a left. The trail runs through my favorite single section on the island, a dark wooded area that looks the same whether traversed in the dead of winter of the dog days of August. Half a mile after the intersection, the trail reaches the summit of Bernard Mountain.

The only realistic return is to retrace your steps. Have fun, but don't cut your own trail.

A cedar post marks the start of the West Ledge Trail on Western Mountain Road

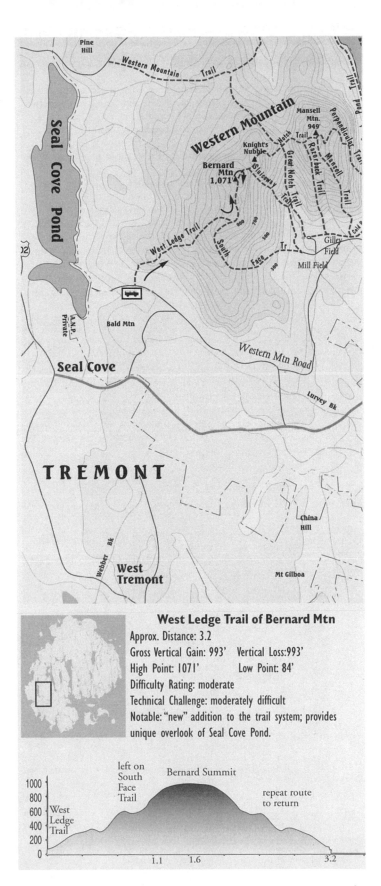

West Ledge Trail of Bernard Mtn

Approx. Distance: 3.2

Gross Vertical Gain: 993'   Vertical Loss: 993'

High Point: 1071'   Low Point: 84'

Difficulty Rating: moderate

Technical Challenge: moderately difficult

Notable: "new" addition to the trail system; provides unique overlook of Seal Cove Pond.

Being at Echo Lake Beach during the summertime might just make you want to get away from it. The Beech Cliffs hike provides a reprieve from the beach, and it offers super views of both Echo Lake and much of the western side of the island. The short but steep trail begins from the corner of the parking lot closest to the stilted cottage. (If you are walking up the stairs leading away from the beach bear right along the thin asphalt sidewalk as you near the parking area.)

A sign post marks the path. As it approaches the cliffs the park service has posted a warning sign that all hikers should heed: the trail climbs the steep side of Beech Cliffs over ladders and steep terrain, so beware![1]

The trail cuts to the left of the perpendicular wall that rises over Echo Lake. It rises intensely, but stairs help placate the abrupt nature of the rise. After passing through the ravine filled with stairs, ladders, and supporting cables, most hikers will reach the ridge quickly. The beach appears to lie directly below the cliffs. Acadia and St. Sauveur Mtns rise to the east with Somes Sound and Sargent Mtn behind them.

To the south the island's Southwest Peninsula extends into the ocean. To the west the Beech Mountain fire lookout tower[2] peers across long views of not only the island but the Gulf of Maine, extending for miles. The trail along this spine leads not only to Beech Cliffs on the right, but also to Canada Cliffs to the left.

Both offer similar views of the area, but the Beech Cliffs end offers some obstructed views of Long Pond and better overall views of Echo Lake. Unfortunately, no trail runs back to Echo Lake Beach gradually.[3]

Hikers must return via the trail they took to the top. The slow pace associated with hiking down extremely steep grades will make the return trip at least as long as the hike to the top. Fine sand, warm water, and many, many screaming kids await your return to the beach.

Beech Cliffs rise over Echo Lake

---

1. The CCC built this trail in the 1930s with the following goals in mind: to make it as narrow and unobtrusive as possible without compromising any degree of safety. The Beech Cliffs Ladder Trail was one of the CCC's last projects; officials felt it was also one of its finest. It achieved many goals of its planners and designers.

2. Also built by the CCC.

3. This is only true because a trail that ran south past Canada Cliffs and down the ridge into Canada Hollow then looped back around to the Echo Lake parking area is now "abandoned." This is one of only a few instances of a CCC-built trail being abandoned; backing your way *down* any ladder trail or cliff trail is definitely more harrowing than going up so be careful!

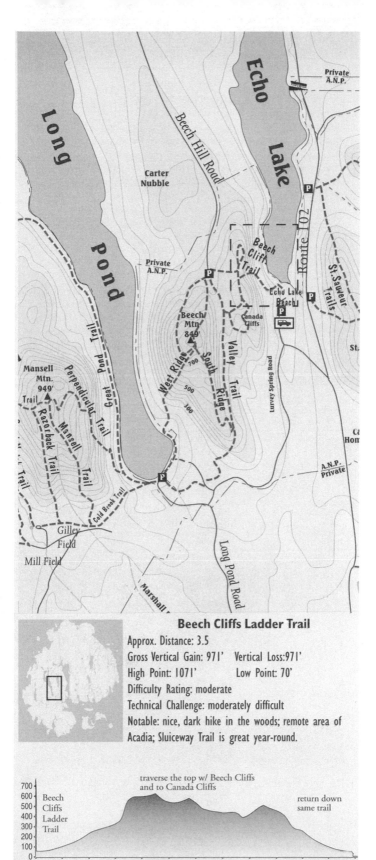

Beech Cliffs Ladder Trail

Approx. Distance: 3.5

Gross Vertical Gain: 971'   Vertical Loss: 971'

High Point: 1071'   Low Point: 70'

Difficulty Rating: moderate

Technical Challenge: moderately difficult

Notable: nice, dark hike in the woods; remote area of Acadia; Sluiceway Trail is great year-round.

traverse the top w/ Beech Cliffs
and to Canada Cliffs

Beech
Cliffs
Ladder
Trail

return down
same trail

Beech Mountain has at least one unique characteristic among all of the mountains on Mount Desert Island: it has a fire tower on its peak (let's not forget the plush rest rooms either).

In the old days (the mid-1800s) Southwest Harbor was the port of entry for most of the early tourists to the island. Defile Mountain, as Beech was then known, served as one of the first hikes the earliest generation of Rusticators would take.[1]

This original route connected this path to Southwest Harbor. Today, Friends of Acadia's Village Trails Connector Committee has made restoration of this connection a priority.

Remnants of four trails run up Beech Mountain, but the fastest way to the top, as well as one of the most popular, starts at the end of Beech Hill Road (the Beech Mountain fire road). A parking area lies at the extreme southern end of the road. The trails to the fire tower start from the same side of the road as the parking lot.

One trail extends from the northern corner of the lot but quickly splits in two. Follow the trail to the right. As it bends around the north side of Beech Mtn and reaches the west face it offers some of the best views available of Long Pond. Straight across the pond the sheer east face of Mansell Mtn rises from water level. (hike 4-3 describes The Perpendicular Trail which climbs this steep face)

The flat southwest peninsula of the island extends into the ocean to the south. As the trail nears the top it reaches the south side of Beech from where the Cranberry Isles and beyond appear.

Although a 'retired' fire look-out, volunteer personnel still occasionally post watch. The short trail back to the parking area begins near the fire tower, marked by a sign post. The trail drops quickly from this crossroads, and views of St. Sauveur and Acadia Mtns flash by as you descend. The upper rim of the Beech and Canada Cliffs area stretches directly to the east. To the north a much wider view appears. The trail drops into the woods and reaches the first intersection just yards from the parking area.

The ugly fire tower appear Pagoda-like as hikers approach from the South Ridge Trail

---

1. According to the book *Trails of History*, the rusticators consisted of "the wandering artist, the roving collegian (who) bivouacked the shore, (and) the pilgrim from stifled cities renewing his jaded strength in the mighty life of nature."

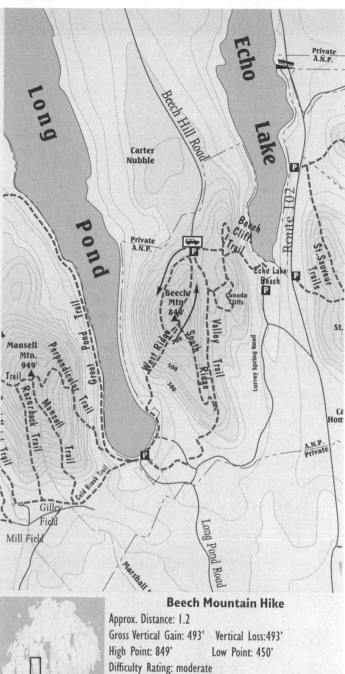

Beech Mountain Hike

Approx. Distance: 1.2
Gross Vertical Gain: 493'   Vertical Loss:493'
High Point: 849'   Low Point: 450'
Difficulty Rating: moderate
Technical Challenge: medium
Notable: quick, relatively easy loop to scenic mountain top.

Beech Mtn summit/firetower

stay to the right on trail from parking lot

descend on north ridge trail of Beech

900
800
700
600
500
400

Canada Cliffs and Beech Cliffs rise over the western shore of Echo Lake and have a long history. First built as a logging road in the 1800s, The Rusticators followed the road through Canada Hollow in their buckboards.

Today, hikers can access this long cliff from the Beech Hill Road parking area. The trail begins by heading in the same direction as the road, dropping gradually over a wide course.

The trail bends left and drops into low, wet areas where small sections of cedar bogwalks help provide dry passage. Away from the bogwalks the trail winds around the back side of the cliffs, passing over stretches of a woodland path that has remained in remarkably good condition. A sign post marks a trail split, but this split is arbitrary; the trails rejoin atop Canada Cliffs. Nears the cliff's face, the ridge appear ahead and the footing changes to smooth rock. The trail runs along the area known as Canada Cliffs and parallels the south shore of Echo Lake.

Beech Cliffs extends ahead. The trail along the Beech Cliffs hugs the edge of the cliffs and looks straight down at Echo Lake below. Several informal trails make their way over the popular cliff area, but they all start near a cedar post which marks the short drop back to the parking area on Beech Hill Road. From the cedar post the trail drops for approximately a quarter mile to the parking area. The short trail could just as well serve as an ultra-short hike in itself to the cliffs area.

Chief Planner for the CCC, Ben Breeze wrote the following on the Beech Cliffs Trail from Beech Hill Road:

It seems that most every trail in Acadia is delightful, but there are other considerations that enter into the actual worth of the trails in the park and perhaps most important from an economical viewpoint is the availability of the trail - the total man days that are spent in travel on the trail during a season. The Beech Cliff's trail does have, aside from its delightfulness, a decided advantage in its ready accessibility and from the start of construction has met with a steadily growing patronage of its beauties. The secret of this success is aside from inherent worth, the fact that the impatient, mile a minute public gets a quick return on the small efforts he expends to travel this trail. It appeals to him to 'hoof it' for only ten minutes to reach a superb eminence such as Beech Cliffs and to see unfolded the expanse of half the island...The main point to be made is that the most used trails are those where a round trip of half an hour to an hour, starting from a motor parking center if possible and of course the motor parking base which commands two or three such scenic loops is in direct proportion more popular...When the work...is done, it will be a major improvement to the Park, and through the Park to the public, will have been accomplished, and one that will be permanent."[1]

Knuckles a.k.a. Pinto checks out some exposed roots on the Canada Hollow section leading to Canada Cliffs.

1.Beech Cliffs Trail Report, Records of the NPS, RG 79, National Archives, Waltham, MA

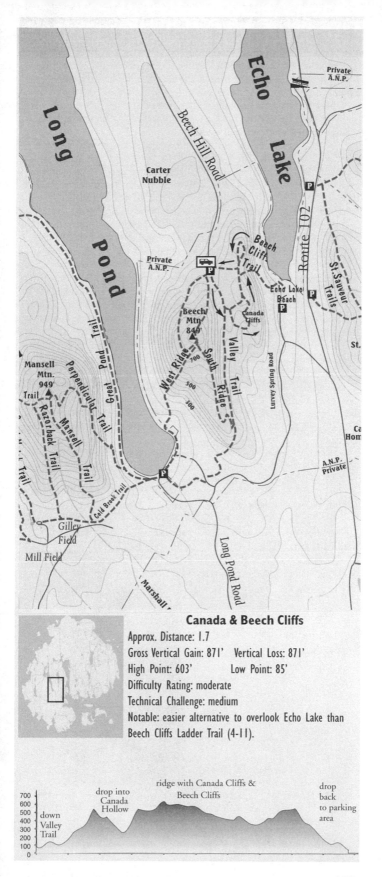

Canada & Beech Cliffs

Approx. Distance: 1.7
Gross Vertical Gain: 871'   Vertical Loss: 871'
High Point: 603'   Low Point: 85'
Difficulty Rating: moderate
Technical Challenge: medium
Notable: easier alternative to overlook Echo Lake than
Beech Cliffs Ladder Trail (4-11).

Whenever I manage to get myself to the 'backside' of the island, I consider it an extra special treat to start any hike that begins at the Long Pond pump house.

This loop up Beech Mountain is no exception.

Start by heading along the Long Pond trail that runs up the east side of the pond (away from the pump house).

This trail runs along the east side of Long Pond for a short, sweet trip past two private homes before it veers up the steep southwest side of Beech Mountain. This trail runs unabashedly across the contours, rapidly gaining elevation and offering views of Long Pond, Southwest Harbor, and the ocean beyond MDI's southwest lobe. Perhaps the most notable view is the Great Pond Trail (hike 4-1) running along the west coast of Long Pond.[1]

This rough trail offers no rest for the weary as it climbs over 900 feet in less than .75mi. Toward the top, the trail levels slightly and bends to the right before merging with the Beech Mountain West Ridge Trail (hike 4-11). Take a right along the wider, more worn path. You will pass two restrooms on the right before bouldering over large granite folds as the trail rises to the fire tower.

It is obvious why this peak would house such a tower. The panorama is incredible. The sun reflects off the tower's glass and it can appear as a ball of fire to Cadillac sunset watchers.

To the east, the ridge containing Canada Cliffs and Beech Cliffs (hikes 4-13 and 4-9) appears. Further east, the steep sides of St.Sauveur and Acadia Mountains create the western shore of Somes Sound's *fjord*.

Continue this loop by heading due south along the trail marked only by blue paint swatches. The trail drops smoothly over granite and wooded surfaces, offering wide views of the Cranberry Isles, Northeast Harbor, the mouth of the sound, and MDI's southern coast from Southwest Harbor to Manset and beyond.

The trail bends to the left just before two old steps rise to an *unmarked* lookout. This next section of trail drops over one of the most scenic stretches of rustic trail in the entire system.[2]

The sculpted trail contains multiple switchbacks that lessen the steep drop as the trail descends a coniferous grove.

The trail intersects with the Valley Trail. Take a right. The trail continues its switchbacks, emerging from thick woods revealing more vistas to the south and west. The trail drops back into woods as is levels.

You will cross a gravel road. The trail continues across and to the left, dropping along a wide, smooth surface back to the starting point at Long Pond.

This is me on one of my favorite trail stretches with my hounds, Tucker, Niblet, and Pinto

---

1. This shore trail built by the CCC required extraordinary amounts of labor and capital (to pay for the extensive stone work and back fill); see *Trails of History* for the whole story.

2. A poster has been made of one short staircase along this section.

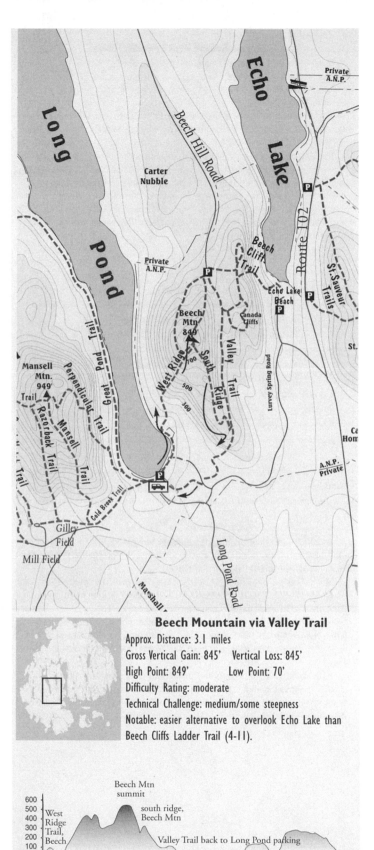

Beech Mountain via Valley Trail

Approx. Distance: 3.1 miles

Gross Vertical Gain: 845'   Vertical Loss: 845'

High Point: 849'   Low Point: 70'

Difficulty Rating: moderate

Technical Challenge: medium/some steepness

Notable: easier alternative to overlook Echo Lake than Beech Cliffs Ladder Trail (4-11).

V. Somes Sound and Seawall Hikes

Three peaks (maybe four, depending on your opinion) rise along the shore of Somes Sound on the island's west side. Of these three, Acadia Mtn receives the most foot traffic, evidenced by the trail appearing worn into the smooth rock surfaces.

Further south, as Valley cove, the island's steepest cliff looms over the cove where access to Acadia Mtn, as well as hikes up St.Sauveur, Valley Peak, and Flying Mtn start.

The Southwest lobe of Mount Desert Island contains the final two hikes of this region. Almost none of the land in this area rises above 100 feet over sea level. Flat, easy hiking results, yet the scenery remains interesting.

The coasts's effects show clearly on each of the hikes.

Also located nearby are the Hio Road, a flat two mile fire road stretching across the Southwest lobe, and Bass Harbor Head Lighthouse, one of the most photographed spots on the island.

Hike	Name	Parking	Level
5-1	Acadia & St.Sauveur Mt	parking on Rte 102	moderate +
5-3	Valley Cove & Peak	Valley Cove parking	difficult
5-5	Flying Mountain	Valley Cove parking	moderate
5-7	Wonderland	102A parking	easy
5-9	Ship Harbor	102A parking	easy

Directions to Parking

Acadia Mtn parking: on Rte 102 south of Somesville, a park service sign marks parking on the right, while a sign post at a set of granite stairs marks the trail on the opposite side of the road.

Valley Cove parking: further south on Rte 102, past the food mart, take a left on Fernald Point Road; follow the road just under a mile to the park service signs marking the Valley Cove parking area on the left.

Wonderland: even further south on 102, after going through Southwest Harbor, take a left on 102A. After about three miles, you'll pass the natural sea wall. A park service sign will mark the Wonderland parking area on the left.

Ship Harbor: located one mile further south than Wonderland.

The Hio Road: park at the Amphitheater lot on loop C in the Seawall Campground; or access the hike from Route 102, south of Southwest Harbor where Bass Harbor Marsh flows under the road on the other side of the heath.

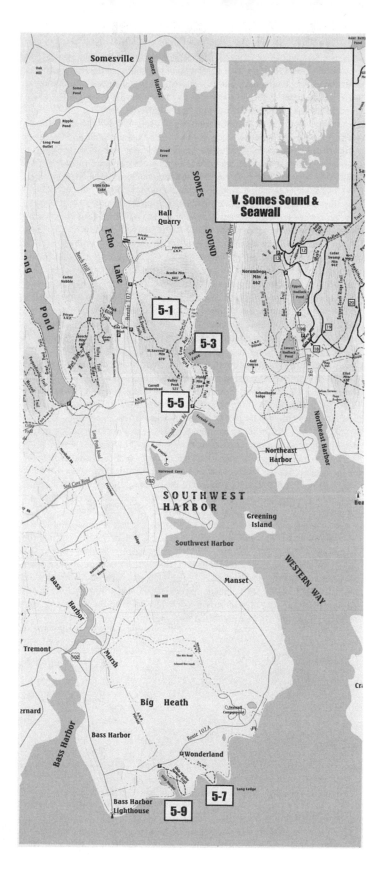

V. Somes Sound & Seawall

Acadia Mountain rises over central Somes Sound. Like the other peaks near the sound, Acadia tops out at a relatively low height but offers wide views of the area. Throughout the island's history Acadia Mountain has been popular although for different reasons during different eras.[1]

Today it seems that Acadia Mountain's treasures are for hikers who are seeking a walk over an ocean-side mountain. Cairns and signposts effectively mark the trail, and the path actually appears worn into the rocks in places, a testament to its popularity. Acadia Mountain's ridge runs east to west rather than north to south as the rest of the mountains on the island do. Most maps show the trails near the parking area incorrectly.

The trail from the parking lot splits after two-tenths of a mile of steady rising. Take the left turn toward Acadia Mtn. The trail drops casually through damp, moss-covered woods before it crosses a fire road. Steep rises characterize the trail up Acadia, although several flat stretches offer respites.

Like Pemetic Mountain on the island's east side, Acadia Mountain actually has two peaks. The first, at 681 feet, is the higher. The second, a nubble that rises to 646 feet, offers superior vistas.

The west side of the island comes into view while Somes Sound stretches to the north, east, and south. Norumbega Mtn rises directly across the water, separated by The Narrows. Sargeant Drive runs along the edge of the water below Norumbega and is visible from Acadia Mountain. Northeast Harbor appears further down the sound.

The eastern side of Acadia Mtn drops in sharp spurts over stretches of smooth rock. In straight ahead fashion the trail drops over 600 feet in less than half a mile. Man O'War Brook occupies the valley between Acadia Mtn and Mt. St. Sauveur.[2] A short trail of stone stairs leads to the small waterfall this brook crosses near its mouth at Somes Sound.

Ahead, this hike reaches an intersection. The fire road leads back to the parking area to the right. St.Sauveur Mtn lies straight ahead.

The trail up St.Sauveur's east face rises steeply. Although similar in grade to the hike up Acadia, the footing along St.Sauveur's east face makes the hiking much more difficult. The narrow trail winds along the eastern side of the mountain where erosion has bared much of the surface. Near St.Sauveur's peak good views of the sound appear, including Valley Cove. Unfortunately the area around the top of St.Sauveur can be confusing. The best views appear away from the summit. (You will be hard pressed to see much of anything from the sign marking the top.)

To return to the car follow the trail to the right from the summit signpost back toward Rte 102 and the Acadia Mtn parking area. Bear to the right at the next sign post as well. The descent stretches 1.1 miles offering scenic woods along a nice trail. The trail revisits the first intersection; the parking lot lies less than a quarter mile to the left.

Acadia Mountain provides the backdrop to this scene from Sargeant's Drive.

1. For many years there was believed to be a buried trove of gold on the side of Acadia. The cellars of *Gold Digger's Glen* are still visible in the woods near the Man O'War Brook fire road.

2. Named for the British war ships that used the waters to replenish their drinking water supplies during MDI's long history of wars and settlers, many tales and legends surround Man O'War Brook. See *Trails of History* for the whole story.

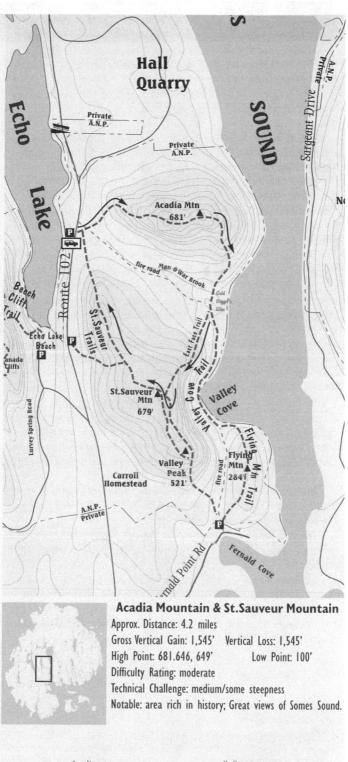

Hall Quarry

Echo Lake

SOUND

Sargent Drive

Private A.N.P.

Private A.N.P.

Private A.N.P.

No

Acadia Mtn 681'

fire road Man O War Brook

Gold Digger's Glen

Route 102

Beach Cliff Trail

East Face Trail

Echo Lake Beach

Canada Cliffs

St. Sauveur Trails

Valley Cove Trail

Valley Cove

St. Sauveur Mtn 679'

Lurvey Spring Road

Flying Mtn Trail

Valley Peak 521'

Flying Mtn 284'

Carroll Homestead

fire road

A.N.P. Private

P

Fernald Point Rd

Fernald Cove

Acadia Mountain & St. Sauveur Mountain

Approx. Distance: 4.2 miles

Gross Vertical Gain: 1,545' Vertical Loss: 1,545'

High Point: 681.646, 649' Low Point: 100'

Difficulty Rating: moderate

Technical Challenge: medium/some steepness

Notable: area rich in history; Great views of Somes Sound.

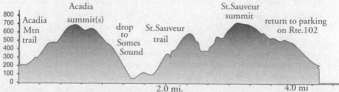

Acadia Mtn trail | Acadia summit(s) | drop to Somes Sound | St. Sauveur trail | St. Sauveur summit | return to parking on Rte.102

800 700 600 500 400 300 200 100 0

2.0 mi. 4.0 mi

Located near the site of the original Jesuit Colony of 1613 at the end of Fernald Point Rd. (the first left off Route 102 after Echo Lake) ANP provides trails to hikers and moorings to sailors.

If hikers choose the Flying Mountain option after hiking Valley Peak and St.Sauveur, the gross vertical on this hike adds up to 1,424 feet!

Start this hike by walking down the gravel road about 75 yards and take a left at the first cedar post. This trail runs steeply up to the top of Valley Peak. I really enjoy this woodland, rustic trail.

Valley Peak is basically a part of St.Sauveur Mountain. No real post marks Valley Peak; rather, the trail simply continues slicing between low-bush blueberries toward St.Sauveur. The views of Somes Sound are excellent along this ridge and trail, and in my opinion are superior (and definitely less crowded) than those available from Acadia Mountain. The straight-down view of Valley Cove visible from near the top of St.Sauveur may be the best scene of the whole hike.

The hike continues over St.Sauveur. It bears to the right along this mountain's sea-side ridge. Once it starts dropping, the descent is steep along the northeast face of the mountain (same as the ascent in hike 5-1).

Take a right at the intersection at the bottom (although a quick diversion lies straight ahead: the small Man O'War waterfall). Valley Cove Trail was the final trail project of the CCC during the 1930s, and one could argue that they did not quite finish this project.[1]

The Valley Cove Shore Trail crosses several small streams as it cuts woodland style to the edge of the sound. Along the shore, this trail's character changes. More than 600 stairs of cut stone and granite form precise sections of the trail as it runs across a haphazard landscape. It passes below Eagle Cliff (formerly known as Thunder Cliff) arguably the island's most sheer and precipitous.[2]

The staircases traverse a rugged rock slide beneath the cliff. Valley Cove appears ahead. Closes to the cove, the stairs end, making the final stretch of this hike difficult.

The trail levels as it reaches the Valley Cove Fire Road. Low tide reveals a large cobble beach where swimming can be tolerable in the summer.

To return to the parking area from this point, take a right and follow the fire road. To add another small mountain to this route, continue straight ahead. A sign post marks the trail leading to the top of Flying Mountain, and better yet, the entire next hike in this book describes that mountain, so turn the page...

---

1. Designed to connect the Valley Cove Fire Road and the Man O'War Brook Fire Road at their respective ends, both seem somehow incomplete with respect to the rest of the well-built trail, wide enough, as planned, for use in fighting fires.

2. Perhaps the most renowned legend regarding this area of MDI offers an origin of St.Sauveur Mountain's former name, Dog Mountain. A witch was said to have thrown her own dogs over this cliff in some sort of bizarre ritual. Neighbors later shot this woman's cat with a silver bullet. Although absent from the event, the witch cried out when her cat was shot, took to her bed, and died; the neighbors succeeded in their plan of ridding themselves of a witch.

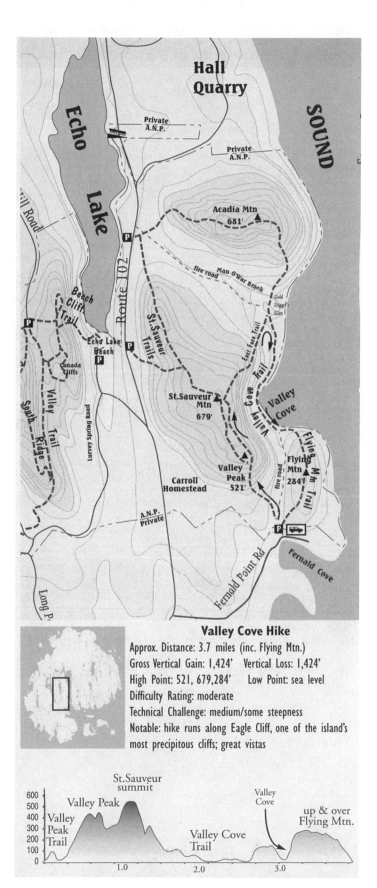

Valley Cove Hike

Approx. Distance: 3.7 miles (inc. Flying Mtn.)

Gross Vertical Gain: 1,424'   Vertical Loss: 1,424'

High Point: 521, 679,284'   Low Point: sea level

Difficulty Rating: moderate

Technical Challenge: medium/some steepness

Notable: hike runs along Eagle Cliff, one of the island's most precipitous cliffs; great vistas

Flying Mtn shares the parking area with the Valley Cove hike (5-3).

Flying Mountain stands as the most moderate hike in the Valley Cove area. It offers superb vistas of the western side of Somes Sound. For a mountain that rises only 284 feet above the sea level the views are tremendous. The top lies less than a quarter mile from the parking area.

Named by the Abnaki who felt the small mountain appeared to have flown off its neighbor 'Dog Mountain' (now known as St.Sauveur Mtn), Flying Mountain has a rich history.[1]

Brief in length, the hike offers quiet overlooks of the immediate area as well as good views of most of Somes Sound and parts of the east side across the sound.

A cedar post marks the Flying Mtn Trail from the parking area. Just into the woods the trail splits; keep to the right. The left-option looks inviting, but don't follow it. The trail needs some maintenance work, but its brevity brings you to the top after only two-tenths of a mile.

The trail continues over the rocky top, and the best views appear from the back side of this hike. Several overlooks provide nice places to view the sound, Sargeant Drive along the opposite side, Norumbega Mtn rising over the road, and Sargent Mtn rising high to the northeast behind Norumbega. Green fields stretch along the shoreline below, and boaters make their way over the waters during most of the tourist seasons. The Cranberry Isles separate the sound from the Atlantic Ocean.

The hike continues down, cascading over rocky ground, passing several other nice overlooks on the right side of the trail. Exposed roots makes the hiking difficult, especially on the steepest descents. The trail reaches the rocky beach at Valley Cove where Valley Peak and St. Sauveur Mtn rise along the edge. Straight ahead the Valley Cove Trail continues alongside the sound (see hike 5-3).

From the beach, the steep "Dog Mountain" cliff of St. Sauveur Mtn appears. This cliff stands as probably the steepest on the entire island. Further right, St. Sauveur Mtn stretches, and Valley Peak extends to the left. The cove houses two courtesy moorings provided by the park service. The parking area lies up the road less than a half-mile to the left.

Left to right, Flying Mountain, Valley Peak, and St.Sauveur Mountain across Somes Sound

---

1.A history *too* long to tell here. See the book *Trails of History* for a series of facts and tales about Flying Mountain.

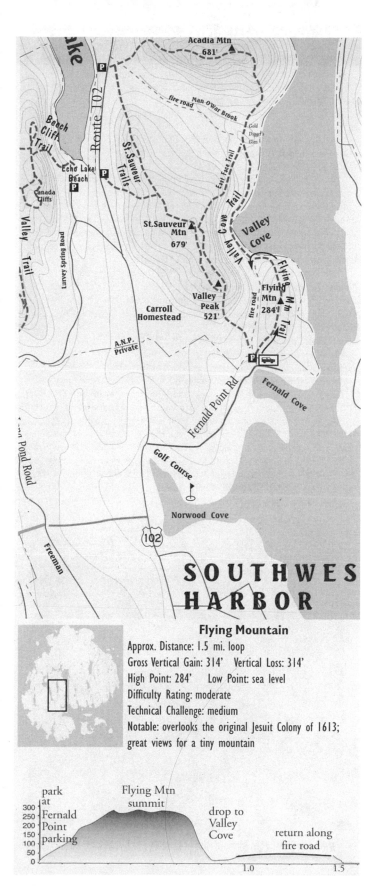

SOUTHWES HARBOR

Flying Mountain

Approx. Distance: 1.5 mi. loop
Gross Vertical Gain: 314'   Vertical Loss: 314'
High Point: 284'   Low Point: sea level
Difficulty Rating: moderate
Technical Challenge: medium
Notable: overlooks the original Jesuit Colony of 1613;
great views for a tiny mountain

A small peninsula stretches into the sea between Southwest Harbor and the village of Bass Harbor. This peninsula's topography contrasts with Mount Desert Island's generally mountainous features. At best, the local coastline along the Seawall area of Acadia mimics the Ocean Drive area at perhaps one-third scale.

For this reason the Wonderland area provides a pleasant, uncrowded diversion, and virtually anyone can enjoy the wide, spacious, and well maintained fire road this hike describes.

Route 102A runs along the eastern shoreline of the area known as Seawall. It passes within feet of the ocean in places along the naturally occurring seawall. Beyond the Seawall Campground (one of two park service campgrounds on the island) 102A heads toward the Bass Harbor Lighthouse. The Big Heath a wet, marshy area occupies most of the acreage in the central part of this peninsula and lies to the right of the road. The heath connects to the north with the Bass Harbor Marsh, another wetland.

The distinctive brown park service sign with white lettering marks the Wonderland parking area. A wide gravel path leads into the woods from the parking lot. The path itself leads directly to a cobble beach facing Bennets Cove. The Duck Islands appear to the southeast, while Great Cranberry Island grabs the eye to the northeast.

A small loop at the end of the gravel path brings hikers to a cobble beach where exploration can be both interesting and scenic. Closer to the water, moss luxuriates over the trees and ground. The lush green of the forest abuts the white, round-stoned beaches. A scaled down version of the rocky Maine coast forms the shoreline in the area, and it stretches far in both directions.

The hike returns to the parking area via the gravel path. Various short narrow trails protrude from the gravel path. These trails provide excellent quiet areas ideal for short wanderings from the fire road. Sturdy, squat pine trees grow in the sand, and native mosses grow on their branches and trunks in this low-lying area. Each trail's brevity precludes hikers from getting "lost," but the trails do provide areas of escape from the main trail. None of these trails seems to head anywhere in particular.

Niblet perching in one of the many twisted trees at Wonderland

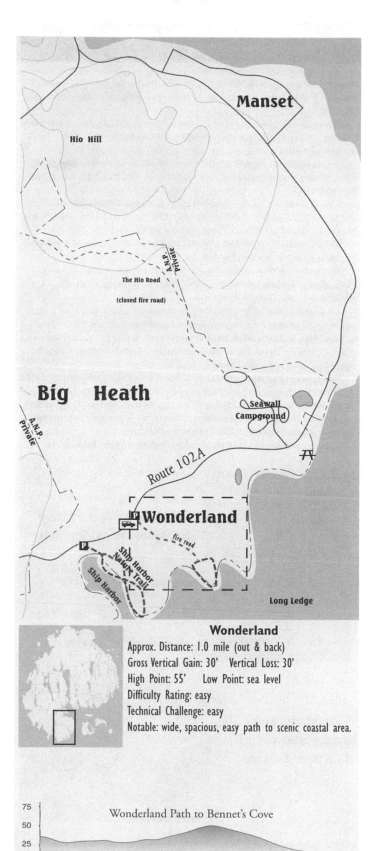

Manset

Hio Hill

A.N.P. Private

The Hio Road
(closed fire road)

Big Heath

A.N.P. Private

Seawall Campground

Route 102A

Wonderland

fire road

P

Ship Harbor Nature Trail

Ship Harbor

Long Ledge

Wonderland

Approx. Distance: 1.0 mile (out & back)
Gross Vertical Gain: 30'   Vertical Loss: 30'
High Point: 55'   Low Point: sea level
Difficulty Rating: easy
Technical Challenge: easy
Notable: wide, spacious, easy path to scenic coastal area.

Wonderland Path to Bennet's Cove

75
50
25
0

Ship Harbor cuts into the island's southwest peninsula between the Wonderland area and the Bass Harbor Lighthouse. The nature trail that forms a figure-eight through the area provides a super hike along and around the quiet shoreline.[1]

On my annual quest to hike each and every trail at least once a year every year (it is harder than it sounds) I missed Ship Harbor in 1998 (but I got it on New Year's Day, 1999).

Sure and steady footing covers ninety percent of this hike. Sound construction and good maintenance keeps the trail in fine shape despite a steady flow of hikers.

The trail forms a figure-eight through the woods. Following the trail to the right, it approaches the shore quickly, running closer to the water than the Ocean Drive Trail (hike 2-9) does on the island's east side. This allows hikers to look nearly straight down into the shallow harbor. Sunny days expose the harbor's sandy, inviting bottom.

Occasional roots and rocks can slow hiking in some places. Outgoing tides, visible from the path, compete with waves to create a relaxing, whooshing sound of water over rocks.

The outer points of Ship Harbor provide numerous choice picnic spots, just over half a mile from the car. A cool sea breeze freshens the warmest summer days. Flat, smooth rocks and grassy areas abound. A sign gives hikers a brief history of the wreck of the Grand Design, an Irish schooner that ran aground at Ship Harbor in the early 1600's.

Many islands appear to the east, including the Duck Islands to the south and Great Cranberry Island to the northeast. The return trip through the woods offers the same atmosphere of the Wonderland Hike, although thicker foliage grows in the Ship Harbor area. Moss grows in the moist environment beneath the spruces, cedars, and balsams in the area.

Hikers can return via the inland route, completing the figure-eight.

The Bass Harbor Head Lighthouse located just south of Ship Harbor

Ship Harbor's narrow opening appears in this classic Maine Coast photo

---

1. The CCC performed work on the Ship Harbor area during the 1930s; much of it, however, occurred on the side of the harbor that is largely unused today.

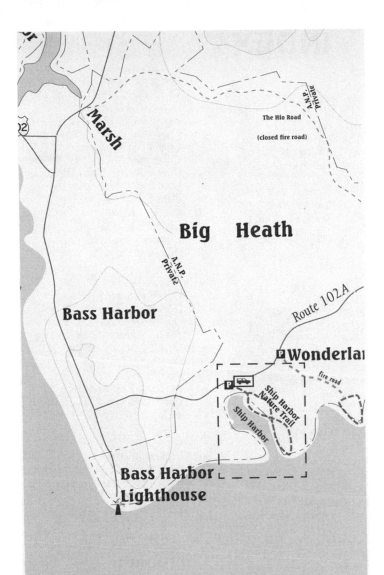

Marsh

The Hio Road

(closed fire road)

A.N.P. Private

Big Heath

A.N.P. Private

Bass Harbor

Route 102A

Wonderlaı

P

P

fire road

Ship Harbor Nature Trail

Ship Harbor

Ship Harbor

Bass Harbor Lighthouse

Ship Harbor

Approx. Distance: 1.3 mile figure-eight
Gross Vertical Gain: 180'   Vertical Loss: 180'
High Point: 45'   Low Point: sea level
Difficulty Rating: easy
Technical Challenge: easy
Notable: easy to follow nature trail; very scenic; trail goes to historic site.

Ship Harbor Nature Trail

right turn from parking area

dip along Harbor

75
50
25
0

1.0

INDEX

GLOSSARY

Acadia Mountain Trail highly popular; steep but basic hiking; trail is very worn even over the rocky areas.

Amphitheater Trail continuation of Little Harbor Brook trail; runs along stream, below an enormous cobble bridge; rocky!

Asticou Trail connects the Jordan Pond area to Brown Mountain

Bald Peak steep; scales the sheer east side of Bald Peak; overlooks Somes Sound and Northeast Harbor; generally good footing over smooth rock.

Bar Island connects Bar Harbor to Bar Island at low tide.

Beachcroft Path rocky but well-laid trail that skirts the west face of Huguenot Head; connects to Champlain.

Bear Brook Trail steep but smooth; a.k.a Champlain's North Ridge.

Beech Cliffs Ladder Trail short, steep trail overlooking Echo Lake.

Beech Mtn Trail short, direct route to top of Beech Mtn

Beech Mtn West Ridge steep trail with good views of Mansell.

Beehive short but steep in sections to top of Beehive.

Bernard South Face Trail steep; mostly packed dirt; some loose rock.

Birch Spring Trail section of Sargent South Ridge that connects Cedar Swamp Mountain trail to top section of south ridge.

Bowl Trail connects Champlain South Ridge to Beehive Trail and Sand Beach; runs along small mountain pond that collects runoff from the Great Ridge area; tends to be wet.

Bubbles Trail from Jordan Pond Trail rocky trail that connects to trails up both Bubbles; starts near the four wooden bridges near the Southwest Pass along the Jordan Pond Trail.

Cadillac Cliffs Trail short detour along Gorham Mtn Trail; unique area.

Cadillac Mtn West Face Trail shortest but steepest route up Cadillac; rises over Bubble Pond; rocky surface; connects to South Ridge Trail.

Cadillac North Ridge Trail moderately steep but good trail; runs near the summit road; exposed
trail; good for sight-seeing.

Cadillac South Ridge one of the island's longest trails; much of it exposed; offers great views to the south; crosses Rte 3 at Blackwoods and reaches the ocean via the campground and loop road, 4.4 miles from peak.

Canada Cliffs Trail narrow woodland trail that drops into Canada Hollow then up to cliffs and connects to Beech Cliffs.

Canyon Brook Trail surface varies greatly; swampy area but trail and bridges in good repair.

Carry Trail connects Jordan Pond to Eagle Lake; can be rocky, but in good shape overall.

Cedar Swamp Mtn Trail southernmost section of Sargent South Ridge Trail; offers spectacular views of Penobscot and the valley to the east; connects Asticou Trail to Birch Spring Trail.

Champlain South Ridge (The Great Ridge) long, relatively gradual trail from top of Champlain to Bowl, Beehive, Sand Beach, and Gorham Mtn areas.

Cold Brook Trail with Gilley Trail, connects the bases of Bernard & Mansell Mtns to Great Pond.

Compass Harbor short, flat hike to a secluded harbor. Close to town.

Conner's Nubble Trail short, moderate hike from the South Shore Eagle Lake trail; very scenic peak at low height; connects to North Bubble Trail.

Day Mtn Trail a moderate climb; well maintained; crosses high-use carriage road three times.

Deer Brook Trail steep trail; crosses brook repeatedly; wooded but extremely rocky trail; connections in upper sections to Jordan Cliffs, Penobscot Mtn, Sargent Mtn Pond, and Sargent Mtn.

Dorr Mtn North Ridge Trail starts at loop road and passes over Kebo Mtn, crosses Hemlock Trail, drops, and rises steeply over smooth rock to the top of Dorr.

Dorr Mtn East Face (Emery Path & Schiff Trails) stepped trail; hundreds of granite steps make hiking this steep face relatively simple; offers superb views of Great Meadow area; connects with Ladder Trail to summit.

Eagle Lake Trail see South Shore Eagle Lake Trail.

East Face Champlain connects to Precipice Trail, Bear Brook Trail; often steep and rocky; reaches loop road at a cedar post.

Eliot Mountain from Little Harbor Brook Trail straight and steep through the woods; stone-marked, but piles are small; twisty near the top.

Eliot Mountain from Route 3 damp near the road, but an otherwise excellent, quiet trail; passes cutoff to Thuya Gardens; traverses smooth rock near the top.

Eliot Mountain from the high point of the Asticou Trail again, twisty, through thick woods, but the footing is excellent, and this route offers the best views of the immediate area; easiest to follow Eliot Mtn Trail.

Eliot Mountain from the Map House at end of Asticou Trail cuts straight through extremely thick woods; many exposed roots.

Featherbed Trail steep, rocky, and often wet trail that connects the Featherbed (on Cadillac South Ridge) to the Bubble Pond/Hunters Brook source, and the Pond Trail.

Flying Mtn short trails up and down; trail gets rough as it approaches Valley Cove; nice overlooks of Somes Sound.

Giant Slide Trail one of the most difficult trails on the island, but well worth the effort; rises along brook; trail extends between huge rocks along the bottom of a chasm; often wet; almost cave-like as it passes beneath some rock formations; connection to Grandgent trail and many others.

Gilley Trail combines with Cold Brook Trail to connect Gilley Field to reservoir; curves upward into Western Mtn (toward Pine Hill) and connects to Long Pond Fire Road.

Goat Trail (Norumbega northeast face) steep & challenging trail up Norumbega Mtn from Rte 198; seems like a long half mile...

Gorge Path trail passes through deep gorges on both ends; runs between Cadillac and Dorr, connects to both; beautifully sculpted trail; rock to rock hiking can get difficult.

Gorham Mtn moderate mile long trail up this coastal peak. Connection to Bowl and Beehive area becomes difficult.

Grandgent Trail starts from the Giant Slide Trail above the "Around the Mountain" carriage road; extremely steep and challenging; *the only trail that gets to the top of Gilmore Peak*; drops over the other side of Gilmore and parallels a mountain stream; seldom used trail; to the east, rises along the steep west face of Sargent Mountain.

Great Head Trails moderate system of trails along Newport Cove, the shore of Frenchman Bay, and returning over Great Head or along marsh to Sand Beach.

Great Pond Trail probably the nicest trail along a lake on the island; very few obstacles

Hadlock Brook Trail rocky trail running from north end of Upper Hadlock Pond up the side of Sargent Mtn; roughly parallels Maple Spring Trail; connects to many other Sargent Mtn trails.

Hadlock Pond Trails quiet, narrow trails that run along the edges of Upper and Lower Hadlock Pond; surface along Lower Hadlock is excellent; along Upper Hadlock, much erosion; carriage road offers good alternative.

Hemlock Trail connects Great Meadow area to the Gorge Path; varied trail surfaces and pitches. Mostly rocky.

Hunters Beach Trail narrow trail that leads to a cobble beach where Hunters Brook reaches the ocean.

Hunters Brook Trail narrow, winding trail that parallels Hunters Brook until it rises toward The Triad and Pemetic Mtn.

Kane Path (The Tarn Trail) watershed during periods of heavy rain; scenic, rolling trail.

Jesup Path flat but scenic path through the freshwater marsh known as the Great Meadow; connects to Sieur de Monts Spring area.

Jordan Cliffs Trail skirts the east face of Penobscot; *technical difficulty should be heeded*, but hike is not overly strenuous.

Jordan Pond Trail mostly flat trail. East side is easier hiking; erosion hazards and rocky footing on northwest corner make the trail difficult; boardwalks improve the west side; connects to Deer Brook Trail and many Bubble trails.

Jordan Stream Trail parallels Jordan Stream; footing varies; erosion by stream can make footing poor; incline is always mild; passes below scenic cobble bridge; becomes marshy as it nears Long Pond.

Kebo Mtn Trail part of the Dorr Mtn North Ridge Trail; sharp rise to top of Kebo from the loop road; overlooks golf course; gradually drops down to Hemlock Trail; Dorr North Ridge straight ahead; Hemlock Trail connects to Sieur de Monts Spring area to the right.

Kurt Diederich's Climb another stepped trail up Dorr's east face. Starts at north end of the Tarn; steps allow vertical feet to be covered with ease of walking up hundred of sets of stairs.

Ladder Trail yet another stepped trail up the east face of Dorr; three iron ladders assist hikers over the steepest areas; starts from south end of Tarn.

Little Harbor Brook Trail extends from Route 3 inland for two miles; narrow trail along the brook; connects to Eliot Mtn, Asticou and Amphitheater Trails.

Lower Hadlock Pond Trail interesting and quiet trail around small pond; recent repairs have improved a good trail.

Man O'War Brook Trail steep from the top of Acadia Mtn; zigzags down the side to the waterfall and the fire road.

Mansell Mtn Trail extends from Cold Brook Trail between Mill Field and Gilley Field to the Great Notch; cutoff to Bernard Mtn's Sluiceway Trail about half way up.

Maple Spring Trail long, varied terrain; needle covered at lower levels near north side of Upper Hadlock Pond; crosses "Around the Mountain" loop at impressive bridge; passes the end of the Giant Slide; jagged and rocky as it rises to Maple Spring; reaches the broad, bald southwest side of Sargent and the South Ridge Trail.

Murphy's Lane connects Precipice Trail parking area to Schooner Head Road; pancake flat; runs through dry section of a large swamp; runs along side of Schooner Head Road.

North Bubble Trail moderate, well marked hike up the north ridge of North Bubble; good views of both Eagle Lake and Jordan Pond; connects Conner's Nubble area to South Bubble Trail and Bubbles Trail from Jordan Pond.

Notch Trail (between Bernard and Mansell) root-covered trail that serves as a crossroads to many Western Mountain trails at the Great Notch.

Ocean Drive Trail oft-travelled trail that parallels the coast and Ocean Drive from Sand Beach to Otter Point. Flat and well groomed.

Parkman Mtn Trail from Route 198 parking area; good footing, rises in spurts; bald east face of mountain offers good views; passes a connecting trail to Bald Peak.

Parkman Mtn from the Giant Slide starts (unmarked) at the spot where the Giant Slide Trail first crosses Sargent Brook; veers off to the right; smoothest and most gradual route up Parkman; precedes another marked trail up Parkman.

Parkman Mtn Trail from Maple Spring trail and end of Giant Slide short, steep, and quite rocky; difficult; goes up the backside of Parkman.

Pemetic Mtn. North Ridge varied and steep terrain; cuts across north ridge; connects to all other Pemetic trails; overlooks Bubble Pond.

Pemetic Trail (West Cliff Trail) connects from the Pond Trail's highest point; rises steeply through thick, rocky woods.

Pemetic (Ravine Trail) starts from loop road at Bubble Rock parking area. Steep, rocky trail that skirts small ravine.

Penobscot South Ridge (Jordan Ridge) most difficult section of this trail occurs just after it crosses carriage road; runs mostly along the wide open south ridge of Penobscot Mtn; smooth rock makes up majority of footing.

Perpendicular Trail hundreds of stairs help make the areas steepest trail a bit less arduous; trail's layout sculpted from granite; nice overlooks to the east; connects to Razorback Trail and trail to Knight's Nubble after passing Mansell Mtn.

Pond Trail excellent trail that runs between The Triad and Pemetic Mtn; connects Jordan Pond to these peaks as well as the west face of Cadillac Mtn via the *Featherbed Trail.*

Precipice Trail Acadia's most difficult trail; iron rungs and ladders assist hikers up the sheer east side of Champlain.

Razorback Trail woodland style; steep; mostly over smooth rock; provides excellent views of Western Mountain.

Sargent Mountain North Ridge Trail steep trail that connects the peak of Sargent with about the highest point along the "Around the Mountain" carriage road loop; below, drops steeply to an intersection with the Giant Slide Trail.

Sargent Mountain Pond Trail connects the peaks of Penobscot Mtn and Sargent Mtn; passes the scenic pond that receives runoff from these two mountains and is the origin of several mountain streams.

Sargent Mountain South Ridge Trail starts from the Asticou Trail; one of the island's longest
ridges; offers excellent views; footing is generally excellent; narrow trail cuts up wide open ridges; sections include Cedar Swamp Mtn Trail & Birch Spring Trail; connects with Sargent Mtn Pond Trail and rises to top.

Seaside Path pleasant trail that connects Jordan Pond area to the ocean at Seal Harbor; parallels Stanley Brook Road section of loop road.

Shady Hill Trail (Norumbega's south ridge) long, gradual trail; good footing.

Ship Harbor Nature Trail well groomed and well travelled trail; provides access to the Seawall coastal areas; basic rocks and roots in small amounts.

Shore Path easy walk along the downtown coastline of Frenchman Bay in Bar Harbor; private land open to public access.

Sluiceway Trail steep trail up Bernard; borders a small mountain stream for a while; connectS to other trails at Great Notch.

South Bubble Trail from Bubble Rock parking short and basically easy trail from parking area to noted glacial erratic rock.

South Bubble Trail from intersection of Jordan Pond Trail and Carry Trail steep, strenuous hike up the south ridge of South Bubble; rocky; some iron rungs to assist over the steepest areas.

South Shore Eagle Lake Trail new boardwalk on the Bubble Pond side; trail rocky as it passes in front of Connors Nubble; runs very close to Eagle Lake; passes Conner's Nubble Trail; reaches Eagle Lake carriage road.

St. Sauveur east face trail connects Man O'War Brook Trail and Valley Cove Trail to St. Sauveur peak; steep and strenuous; bends away from the sound to the top.

Strath Eden Path runs along the lower east edge of Kebo Mtn from Hemlock Trail to loop road; recently restored.

Triad Trail from Day Mtn (Van Santvoord Trail) steep, direct trail to Triad's highest point.

Triad Trail relatively spacious woodland style trail .

Valley Cove Shore Trail skirts Valley Cove; stairs help over the steepest sections.

Valley Peak Trail steep and through thick woods; rises in sharp spurts; some sections nice and needle covered; connects to St. Sauveur Mtn.

Van Santvoord Trail see Triad Trail from Day; bronze plaque is set as a memorial at the top.

Western Cliffs Trail of Pemetic Mtn see Pemetic Trails.

Wildwood Dane Trail from Day Mtn steep, narrow trail that drops off the northwest side of Day Mtn; in need of maintenance; disappearing yearly.

Wonderland fire road provides easy access to cobble beaches; small narrow trails extend indefinitely into the woods on the right side of the fire road.

Are you ready for this? A notched log bridge spans a chasm on the Jordan Cliffs Trail (hike 3-19).

COUPONS

COUPON:

FREE DESSERT WITH PURCHASE OF TWO DINNERS AT JACK RUSSELL'S. ONE COUPON PER VISIT. PLEASE CALL FOR RESERVATIONS AT 288.5214

FROM *A WALK IN THE PARK*

COUPON:

10% OFF ANY LUNCH CHECK AT JACK RUSSELL'S BREW PUB, LOCATED AT 102 EDEN STREET, BAR HARBOR. ALCOHOL AND GRATUITY NOT INCLUDED. ONE COUPON PER VISITT. PLEASE CALL FOR RESERVATIONS AT (207)288-5214

FROM *A WALK IN THE PARK*

COUPON:

$5 OFF ANY TEE SHIRT OR HAT AT MAINE COAST BREWING CO., LOCATED AT 102 EDEN STREET IN BAR HARBOR. ONE COUPON PER VISIT.

FROM *A WALK IN THE PARK*

COUPON:

$5 OFF ANY TEE SHIRT OR HAT AT JACK RUSSELL'S., LOCATED AT 102 EDEN STREET, BAR HARBOR . ONE COUPON PER VISIT.

FROM *A WALK IN THE PARK*

COUPON:

10% OFF ANY FOOD PURCHASE AT JACK RUSSELL'S, LOCATED AT 102 EDEN STREET, BAR HARBOR. CALL 288.5214 FOR RESERVATIONS. ALCOHOL AND GRATUITY NOT INCLUDED. ONE COUPON PER VISIT.

FROM *A WALK IN THE PARK*

COUPON:

15% OFF ANY DIRECT PURCHASE FROM PARKMAN PUBLICATIONS (SEE PAGE 143 FOR ORDER FORM). COUPON REQUIRED FOR PURCHASE

FROM *A WALK IN THE PARK*

COUPON:20% OFF DINNER FOR TWO FOR ANYONE BRINGING IN A PICTURE OF THEIR JACK RUSSELL AT JACK RUSSELL'S, LOCATED AT 102 EDEN STREET, BAR HARBOR. CALL 288.5214 FOR RESERVATIONS. ALCOHOL AND GRATUITY NOT INCLUDED. ONE COUPON PER VISIT

FROM *A WALK IN THE PARK*